VERDUN
1916

EXPLORE HISTORY'S MAJOR CONFLICTS WITH
BATTLE STORY

978-0-7524-6196-0 £9.99   978-0-7524-6310-0 £9.99   978-0-7524-7933-0 £9.99

978-0-7524-7977-4 £9.99   978-0-7524-6878-5 £9.99   978-0-7524-7956-9 £9.99

978-0-7524-6202-8 £9.99   978-0-7524-8056-5 £9.99   978-0-7524-6576-0 £9.99

Visit our website and discover thousands of
other History Press books.
www.thehistorypress.co.uk

VERDUN
1916

CHRIS McNAB

'If you haven't seen Verdun, you haven't seen anything of war'.
A French infantryman, quoted in Ousby, *Verdun*

First published 2013
by Spellmount, an imprint of
The History Press
The Mill, Brimscombe Port
Stroud, Gloucestershire, GL5 2QG
www.thehistorypress.co.uk

British Library Cataloguing in Publication Data.
A catalogue record for this book is available from the British Library.

ISBN 978 0 7524 8870 7

Typesetting and origination by The History Press
Printed in Great Britain
Manufacturing managed by Jellyfish Solutions Ltd

CONTENTS

LIST OF
ILLUSTRATIONS

11 A French soldier prepares to throw a grenade, while his comrade prepares the fuse of another. (*The Illustrated War News*, 5 April 1916)

12 Tracking a 6in shell in flight: A French gunner following with his eye a long-range shot. (*The Illustrated War News*, 22 March 1916)

13 The *Poilu's* cup of tea *à l'anglaise* at the front. (*The Illustrated War News*, 5 April 1916)

14 French bayonet charge, 1916. (Author's collection)

15 Battle of Verdun, 21 February 1916–16 December 1916.

16 Fort Douaumont, 1916. (Wikimedia Commons)

17 An angle of the fort against which thousands of German guns hammered in vain. (*The War Budget*, 20 April 1916)

18 French defence work representative of many miles of the French front. (*The Illustrated War News*, 15 March 1916)

19 After a heavy bombardment, the German soldiers attacked Verdun over devastated ground such as this. (*The War Budget*, 30 March 1916)

20 Refugees from bombarded Verdun. (*The Illustrated War News*, 15 March 1916)

21 Verdun and environs: To the right, the cathedral towers mark the city; to the left, a shell is seen bursting. (*The Illustrated War News*, 29 March 1916)

22 The destruction of a French church by German shells: The bombardment of Vaux-Devant-Damloup, near Verdun. (*The Illustrated War News*, 3 May 1916)

23 Wrecked buildings in the village of Douaumont. (*The Illustrated War News*, 15 March 1916)

24 The French forces at Verdun were continually engaged in preparing, emplacing or repairing barbed-wire defences in the landscape. (*The Illustrated War News*, 22 March 1916)

37 Light railways were used by the French for transporting the wounded to a field ambulance. Here we see a stretcher case on a truck. (*The Illustrated War News*, 5 April 1916)

38 'Hecatombs' – Sacrificed to the moloch of Prussian militarism: Massed infantry attacking at Verdun mown down by the French guns. (*The Illustrated War News*, 29 March 1916. Drawn by Frederic de Haenen)

39 A French bivouac in a church in the environs of Verdun. (*The Illustrated War News*, 19 April 1916)

40 Relief column on its way to the frontlines at Verdun. (*The War Budget*, 16 March 1916)

41 French artillery depot behind the Verdun battle zone. (*The Illustrated War News*, 15 March 1916)

42 One of France's famous motor guns in action dropping shells into the German lines 5km (3 miles) away. *(The War Budget*, 16 March 1916)

43 German prisoners at Verdun: One of the batches lined up in a village for General Joffre's inspection. (*The Illustrated War News*, 22 March 1916)

44 German prisoners working under a French guard. (*The Illustrated War News*, 7 June 1916)

45 'The Road-bed' – cartoon depicting the slaughter at Verdun. (*The War Budget*, 30 March 1916. *New York Evening Telegram*)

46 Heavy artillery, such as these siege guns held in reserve, were critical to the French victory at Verdun. (*The Illustrated War News*, 19 April 1916)

47 Supplies of French heavy shells on their way to the firing line: Motor ammunition wagons on the road. (*The Illustrated War News*, 22 March 1916)

48 'The growing pile' – cartoon depicting the effect of defeat at Verdun on 'Germany's hopes'. (*The War Budget*, 16 March 1916. *Montreal Star*)

INTRODUCTION

It is the fate of some towns, cities, regions and even entire nations to have histories written in blood and war. Usually this situation is a by-product of location, the place sitting on some political or social fault line that periodically gives way to violence and upheaval. The area in and around Verdun in northern France is one such place.

The town of Verdun sits some ▓▓▓▓ (140 miles) due east of the French capital, Paris, roughly ▓▓▓▓ (25 miles) from the German border. Its origins stretch back to the fourth century BC, when Celtic tribesmen founded the settlement named Virodunum, on the banks of the River Meuse. The settlement grew steadily over the next 500 years, the Celts then the Romans appreciating its strategic position for controlling one of the Meuse's key crossings, and its convenient location between the towns of Reims and Metz. The Huns also recognised Verdun's inherent advantages, sacking the town comprehensively in AD 450.

If we were to look for the earliest roots of the 1916 battle that is the subject of this book, then the Treaty of Verdun in AD 843 would be a reasonable place to start. The treaty saw the complicated and contentious division of the Carolingian Empire between the three surviving sons of Louis the Pious (r. 814–40). Although this political solution brought a temporary end to the immediate struggles of the Carolingian Civil War, its effect on Verdun itself was to make the town a political ping-pong ball, knocked between the French and the Germans. The town was largely under German authority until 1552, when it was diplomatically acquired for France (along with Metz and Toul) by Henry II (r. 1154–89), although it took more than 100 years for the Germans to acknowledge French sovereignty, as part of the Peace of Westphalia treaties (signed May–October 1648).

By this time, Verdun was also beginning its transformation into a fortified military outpost. Following the construction of a defensive citadel between 1624 and 1636, the great military engineer Sebastien Le Prestre, known as Marshal Vauban, was commissioned by Louis XIV (r. 1643–1715) to transform France's border defences, including those at Verdun, which would act as a protective sentinel across the approaches to Paris. A map from 1695 shows a classic geometric citadel, surrounded by an equally ornate curtain wall, sat astride both banks of the Meuse, although building these structures would drag on well into the eighteenth century.

The reputation of Verdun's defences and defenders was dealt a savage blow in the 1790s, amidst the Revolutionary Wars (1792–1802), when the town surrendered to Prussian forces on 3 September 1792. Although it was reclaimed by French troops just over a month later, Verdun's vulnerability to a determined enemy was apparent. This lesson was reiterated in 1870, during the Franco-Prussian War (1870–71). Following Emperor Napoleon III's initial spirited invasion of the Prussian Rhineland with the 200,000-strong Army of the Rhine, the Prussians quickly began to assert their tactical and technological superiority. A series of progressive French defeats led to the surrender of Verdun, with full military honours, on 8 November 1871; the Prussians would stay in occupation until September 1873. Worse still for France, the final Prussian victory in the war not only led to the creation of a unified, and powerful, united German state in Europe, but France's territorial loss of Alsace and Lorraine to the Germans meant that the Franco-German border was pushed further westwards towards Paris. The Meuse was now the principal physical barrier against a future German invasion and Verdun was a key strongpoint.

Defeat in the Franco-Prussian War galvanised the French to establish a Comité de Défense (Defence Committee), which would oversee the creation of a new chain of fortified border defences, chiefly under the direction of the military engineer Séré de Rivières. The work would continue for several decades, many of the fortifications having to be re-designed during the 1880s and 1890s to respond to new threats from more powerful rifled artillery and high explosives. Nevertheless, by the time a major European war broke out again in 1914, Verdun cast an imposing shadow over the French landscape. It featured a total of nineteen major forts, armed with concrete- and metal-emplaced 155m and 75mm cannon and machine guns, with a total of forty-seven armoured observation posts set about the landscape. The garrison of the Verdun region numbered 65,000 men.

As history now reveals, the global conflict that raged between 1914 and 1918 was one that truly rang the changes in the tactics and strategies of warfare. In the past, when the range and potency of artillery was less and the absence of railways reduced army mobility, massive static defences made a good degree of sense. They acted as breakwaters against which armies would smash themselves, bulwarks to sap the energy from the enemy attempts to advance and claim ground. In the First World War, however, almost every aspect of military operations underwent a revolution. Logistics, air power, artillery, communications, tactical manoeuvre, infantry firepower, command-and-control, uniforms and equipment – everything was modernised by the demands of both the scale of the conflict and the processes of industrialisation inherent in total war. Fortresses such as those at Verdun had an uncertain role in this changing landscape, especially as the offensive became the doctrinal focus of the French high command (see 'The Armies' chapter). What fortresses still provided, however, was both a gathering point for major accumulations of troops, and locations that commanded a very real sense of national pride. It was upon these factors that the German forces, in 1916, would precipitate one of history's most horrific battles. In an engagement of grotesque attrition between February and December 1916, one million men would be casualties, including about 300,000 battlefield deaths. If ever there was a near-perfect demonstration of the brutality inherent in the emerging era of modern warfare, it was to be found at Verdun.

TIMELINE

1914	3–4 August	Germany declares war on France and Belgium
	5–10 September	German invasion of France stopped at the First Battle of the Marne
	September–December	German, British and French forces establish trench networks running from the Channel coast down to Switzerland
1915	January–November	French forces make a series of offensives throughout the year in the Champagne, Artois and Lorraine
	20 June–13 July	The Germans prosecute their Meuse–Argonne offensive. Neither the French nor German attacks change the lines significantly
	16 December	Joffre receives official complaints about the state of the defences at Verdun, and warnings of future German offensives in the region
1916	21 February	The Battle of Verdun begins with a lengthy German preparatory bombardment and an infantry assault
	22 February	Bois des Caures overrun

1916

25 February	Fort Douaumont is captured by the Germans. Pétain takes command of the Verdun sector
4 March	Douaumont village is captured
6 March	Germans push their offensive at Verdun down the left bank of the Meuse
6 March– 9 April	Intense fighting continues at Verdun, focused on places such as Forges, Regnéville, Le Mort-Homme, Fort Vaux, Haucourt and Malancourt
9 April	Germans launch a five-division attack on the left bank of the Meuse, establishing positions on Le Mort-Homme
April	French forces make several counter-attacks, although with little change in the frontlines
30 April	Pétain takes command of Army Group Centre; Nivelle becomes commander of Second Army
June	Heavy fighting in the Thiaumont–Fleury–Souville sector
8 June	Fort Vaux surrenders to the Germans
23 June	German offensive captures the Thiaumont Redoubt
1 July	Anglo-French Somme offensive begins further north, drawing off German reserves from Verdun
24 October	French forces launch a major counter-offensive at Verdun, capturing Thiaumont Redoubt and Farm, Fort Douaumont and several other key locations
2 November	French recapture Fort Vaux
15 December	A new French offensive pushes German forces back to the Bois de Chaume. The Germans have by now lost nearly all their territorial gains at Verdun

Verdun 1916

1917

1918

20–26 August A major French offensive at Verdun makes several more key gains in the sector, plus inflicts heavy losses on the German defenders

26 September A Franco-American offensive in the Meuse–Argonne sector puts the Germans into their final retreat. By October the Germans have lost the Bois des Caures

11 November Armistice signed, bringing war on the Western Front to an end

HISTORICAL BACKGROUND

When war began in August 1914, after a flurry of failed diplomacy and military mobilisation across Europe, it was readily apparent that France was fighting for its survival. For Germany, a modified (1906) version of the 'Schlieffen Plan' – named after its original architect Count Alfred von Schlieffen – had at its heart a rapid and decisive defeat of France. Germany's age-old problem was how best to deal with the possibility of a two-front war between France to the west and Russia to the east. In the revised plan, largely shaped by the German Chief of Staff Helmuth von Moltke, German forces in the east would focus mainly on holding the Russians in place, banking on slow mobilisation of the vast Russian Army to stem any advance from that quarter. At the same time, a German force, five armies strong, would undertake an invasion of France. Here was the crucial strategic ingredient. Germany's only option, if it was to respect the declared neutrality of Belgium and Luxembourg, would be to advance directly against France's fortified border lines between Belgium and Switzerland. Battering through these regions would likely devolve into a slow grind when time was of the essence – France had to be defeated before the full forces of Russian power could be brought to bear in the east. The solution was to use Belgium and Luxembourg as invasion routes into northern France, the hinge of the thrust in the south being just to the north of Verdun. This way the German armies would be able to advance rapidly, bypassing the French border forts and swinging down through France to capture Paris and effectively knock the French quickly out of the war. Schlieffen himself saw this strategy as a 'battle of annihilation':

> A battle of annihilation can be carried out today according to the same plan devised by Hannibal in long forgotten times. The enemy front is not the goal of the principal attack. The mass of the troops and the reserves should not be concentrated against the enemy front; the essential [point] is that the flanks be crushed. The wings should not be sought at the advanced points of the front but rather along the entire depth and extension of the enemy formation. The annihilation is completed through an attack against the enemy's rear... To bring about a decisive and annihilating victory requires an attack against the front and against one or both flanks...
>
> Count Alfred von Schlieffen

The 'attack against the front' would largely be provided by the German Fifth Army, which would strike directly into France proper just below the bend of the Franco-Belgian border. Meanwhile, two further armies – the Sixth and Seventh – would adopt holding positions behind the River Moselle, to prevent French incursions into the German homeland. With the defeat of France complete, the bulk of German forces would then redeploy rapidly to the Eastern Front by rail to fight the now-mobilised Russians.

Military plans have a near surgical neatness on paper that is rarely ever realised so cleanly on the ground. The Schlieffen Plan was no exception, as what should have been a swift French defeat became four years of attrition on a near static Western Front. For a start, the French had a response of their own for the eventuality of war with Germany. Known as Plan XVII, the heart of its aims was to retake Alsace and Lorraine – the loss of these territories had been a thorn in the French psyche since 1871 – and to provide a clear offensive demonstration to the Russian allies, encouraging them to act in the east while France advanced to the Rhine in the west. Note also, however, that the French were not naïve to the possibility that the Germans might attempt an invasion via Belgium. For this reason, the French Fifth Army was deployed in the far north, although the French high command never truly envisaged the scale of the German thrust through the neutral territory. For their part, the Russians planned on an offensive against Germany and Austria-Hungary (Germany's principal ally) in East Prussia, Galicia and Silesia, widely separated fronts that would place additional strains on Russian logistics and mobilisation. The British, for their part, would essentially be reactive to events, planning to provide an expeditionary force in support of France and a violated Belgium.

From 4 August 1914, the validity of the respective European war plans was put to the test. German forces swung en masse into Belgium, attacking the fortified defences protecting Liège the next day. Belgian resistance here was stiffer than expected, and it took until 16 August to subdue all the forts, courtesy of the use of massive 305mm and 420mm siege guns, and resume the advance. Note that the German plan allowed for just six weeks in which the French were to be defeated. During this time, the French had responded with the rapid implementation of Plan XVII. Attacks into Alsace on 7 August brought what appeared to be encouraging results for the French – Altkirch, Thann and Mulhouse (Mülhausen) were captured in short order, the latter with a much-publicised bayonet charge. Yet the offensive soon ran into problems, in the face of German counter-attacks. Mulhouse was lost on 10 August, then recaptured a few days later by a more powerful French push by the First and Second Armies. But by now the German counter-attacks were growing in strength, as the German high command gave the southern operations more weight in the overall context of the Schlieffen Plan. Mulhouse fell back into German hands on the 27th, even as other French offensives against Metz and Neufchâteau in the Ardennes were collapsing in the face of German firepower.

What we now know as the Battle of the Frontiers was, after two weeks of fighting, a costly failure for the French forces. The offensives had been pushed back by the Germans and 300,000 French soldiers were casualties, although the Germans were finally stopped in front of the Verdun–Nancy–Belfort fortresses.

Further north, the Germans were pushing on, although not without problems. Following the defeat of the Liège fortifications, the German First, Second and Third Armies deepened their advance into central Belgium, taking Brussels on 20 August. An attempted encirclement of the Belgian Army had not been realised; the 117,000 men of the Belgian Army managed to slip out of the closing net and retreat to secure fortified positions in Antwerp. Struggling against the German advance were four French armies (from west to east, the Fifth, Ninth, Fourth and Third) plus, on the far left flank, 110,000 men of the British Expeditionary Force (BEF), who had begun to arrive in France on 7 August and who inflicted heavy casualties on the Germans at the Battle of Mons on 23–24 August. Despite such victories, the BEF and the French Fifth Army were unable to contain the combined force of the German First and Second Armies. As Germany pushed down into northern France in late August, Paris itself seemed imperilled and to the casual observer the Schlieffen Plan looked to being unfolding as intended.

Yet behind the scenes, Moltke's vision of a quick French defeat was dissolving. Logistics were starting to fail to keep up with the lengthening advance (a shortage of horses and specialist engineering troops were critical problems, as was the issue of ever greater distance from railheads), and men were becoming exhausted. The German high command also made a serious strategic blunder as they approached the French capital. Not wishing to over-extend their front, the German First and Second Armies swung to the east of Paris, rather than the west, leaving them exposed to an unexpectedly ferocious counter-attack on the Marne.

The Battle of the Marne was one of the critical moments in the early years of the war. Launched on 5 September it effectively stopped the advance of the German First Army and split it from the Second Army further east. The BEF and the French Fifth Army exploited the gap with an attack on the 9th, and in response the German First Army was forced to make a withdrawal back to the Aisne.

Paris was saved, and the strategic and moral nature of the victory was not lost on General (Gen.) Joseph Joffre, a central figure in the French victory:

The completeness of our victory becomes more and more apparent. Everywhere the enemy is in retreat. The Germans are abandoning prisoners, wounded, and material in all directions.

After the heroic efforts displayed by our troops during this formidable battle, which has lasted from the 5th to the 12th of September, all our armies, exhilarated by success, are carrying out a pursuit which is without parallel in its extension.

On our left we have crossed the Aisne below Soissons, thus gaining more than 100 kilometres in six days of battle. In the centre our armies are already to the north of the Marne. Our armies of Lorraine and the Vosges are reaching the frontier.

Our troops, as well as those of our Allies, are admirable in morale, endurance, and ardour. The pursuit will be continued with all our energy. The Government of the Republic may be proud of the army which it has prepared.

General Joseph Joffre, 13 September 1914

The ebullient mood was justified, but the war was about to develop in a way few strategic thinkers would have conceived. Both sides saw the opportunity to outflank the other in the west in the territory between Soissons and the French/Belgian coast. Their attempts to do so became known as the 'Race to the Sea'. Neither side ultimately managed to outflank, but in the process they created a long, static frontline that stretched from the Swiss border to Nieuport on the coast in Flanders. This frontline hardened into the earth in the form of trench positions, manned by the huge volumes of volunteer and regular soldiers now being poured into the Western Front. The Schlieffen Plan, which was meant to be an epic demonstration of German mobile warfare, was now locked into a frontline that would scarcely change significantly for the next three years.

Taking the Offence

Naturally enough for nations eager to secure victory, much effort and huge volumes of blood were expended in attempts to break the deadlock on the Western Front in 1915 and 1916. Offensive action, at least until the Battle of Verdun, was disproportionately weighted in favour of the French and the British. The Germans, during the Race to the Sea, had managed to secure for themselves a good collection of geographically and militarily defensible positions along the frontline, while retaining a large chunk of northern France and most of Belgium. They were also engaged in a major war on the Eastern Front, which in itself was gobbling up thousands of men, so by far the best policy on the Western Front was to establish very strong lines of defence and let the enemy wear himself out on them.

For the French and British a similar policy would have been spiritually intolerable. Thus we see a regular sequence of major Anglo-French offensives (combined or unilateral) conducted throughout 1915. Detailing the development and fighting of each of these offensives is beyond the scope of this book, but a demoralising pattern steadily emerged for the Allies. In many cases, an offensive would begin promisingly, a surging infantry assault pushing across no man's land in the wake of a bludgeoning artillery bombardment. Often the German first-line trenches were penetrated and overcome, but the Germans were masters of recovery and defence in depth. After an initial Allied advance, therefore, the momentum would drain away as the French or British soldiers ran up against strong second-line positions, or were driven back by an elastic counter-attack, often to their start positions. Moreover, the cost of each offensive was horrendous, given the paltry gains made. For example, a French offensive launched in Champagne on 16 February 1915 lasted just over a month and cost 40,000 casualties for just 3km (1.8 miles) of territory gained. Another French push in Artois on 25 September resulted in a further 190,000 casualties for inconsequential results. With the French Army having suffered 1.2 million war casualties by the end of 1915, there was the real danger that the offensive spirit might simply bleed away its soldiery.

So where did Verdun fit into this big picture, from both sides of the frontline? (Note that the actual structure of the French defences at Verdun is described in the next chapter.) Verdun, occupying a bulging salient, was actually one of the most defensible French positions along the entire frontline, although not everyone on the French staff appreciated that fact. In September 1914 German forces had attempted to encircle and cut off the fortified town. This effort came close to success, not only because the German pincers nearly closed around Verdun, but also because Joffre had actually ordered the town to be abandoned. Thankfully for the French, Verdun's commander disobeyed the order. Yet the Germans did succeed in weakening Verdun's defensive integrity. The outlying Fort Troydon and Fort Camp des Romains were destroyed and captured respectively,

DID YOU KNOW?

The Underground Citadel at Verdun featured 4km
(2.5 miles) of passages, set deep beneath the earth. It could
also accommodate 6,000 men, although the
conditions beneath the ground were often
dank and unwholesome.

and two of the main railway lines into Verdun were cut, leaving the town with just a single road and a narrow-gauge railway track from Bar-de-Luc as its main routes of supply from the west. The Germans also managed to capture the Les Éparges ridge, a strategically useful piece of high ground 24km (15 miles) to the south-east of Verdun. A French counter-attack from 17 February 1915 reclaimed much of the ridge, although some eastern parts of the feature remained in German hands almost until the end of the war. Twenty-four kilometres (15 miles) to the west of the town, the elevated Butte de Vauquois was similarly contested. The German capture of the feature brought vigorous French counter-attacks in the early months of 1915, but while infantry combat largely ground to a halt by 4 March, mine warfare continued for months to come, as each side attempted to secure the feature.

While fighting continued around Verdun, the town and its fortresses themselves came in for German attention, chiefly in the form of aerial and artillery bombardment. The latter included a fearsome pounding of Forts Douaumont and Vaux by 420mm howitzers, which succeeded in creating some significant external damage but without disabling critical French gun emplacements. Apart from such fiery interruptions, however, Verdun was actually one of the quieter sectors on the front. This was reflected not only in an encroaching complacency amongst the French garrison, but also in the stripping of many of the fortress' guns to provide artillery for batteries elsewhere. (Both these occurrences are examined in more detail in the following chapter.) The insouciance of the Verdun town itself is summed up perfectly by Verdun historian Alistair Horne:

> The proximity of war and the spasmodic bombardments had reduced the population of Verdun from somewhere under 15,000 to about 3,000. But those that remained had adapted themselves well, and had seldom had it so good. The proprietors of a former music shop now sold tomatoes and tins of sardines to the voracious *poilus* (at a handsome profit); a hotel for travelling salesmen had put up the board but did a brisk business in wine by the barrel, and cheese and oranges were retailed from a disused cinema… At the *Coq Hardi* evenings were as gay as ever before the war. The officers dining there may have looked back with some nostalgia on the peacetime fishing in clear streams and the wonderful *chasses au sanglier* among the oak woods that covered the hills beyond the Meuse, now the forward area, but otherwise life was not disagreeable.
>
> Alistair Horne, *Price of Glory*, pp.46–47

Unknown to the French in Verdun, decisions were being taken within the German high command that would eventually make this relaxed existence nothing but a haunted and shattered memory.

Falkenhayn's Plan

In 1915, with the Schlieffen Plan clearly dead in the water, the German high command began to contemplate its next major strategic move to turn the war in its favour. In December 1915, Erich von Falkenhayn, chief of staff, who had replaced Moltke in September 1914, began writing a lengthy memorandum for Kaiser Wilhelm, in which he outlined the state of the conflict and the route to victory. Falkenhayn, giving priority to the Western Front over the Eastern Front (earning the enmity of many of his peers), identified Britain as Germany's most pressing foe, with its vast industrial resources and the human capacity of its great empire. Falkenhayn laboriously listed the strategic options for taking on Britain, but through circuitous logic arrived at the conclusion that the best strategy was to knock the French out of the war:

> There remains only France… If we succeeded in opening the eyes of her people to the fact that in a military sense they have nothing more to hope for, that breaking point would be reached and England's best sword knocked out of her hand. To achieve that object the uncertain method of a mass breakthrough, in any case beyond our means, is unnecessary. We can probably do enough for our purposes with limited resources. Within our reach behind the French sector of the Western front there are objectives for the retention of which the French General Staff would be compelled to throw in every man they have. If they do so the forces of France will bleed to death.

> Quoted in Horne, *Price of Glory*, p.36

The place chosen to 'bleed' France to death was Verdun. Falkenhayn would have known that the Kaiser's son, the Crown Prince, was leading the German Fifth Army opposite Verdun, so would have banked on a favourable hearing for the plan. Details are uncertain, but it appears that Falkenhayn had an audience with the Kaiser in Potsdam in late December, and managed to gain approval for the campaign via a memorandum that outlined the plan. The action was to be called Operation Gericht – options for translation include 'tribunal', 'judgement'

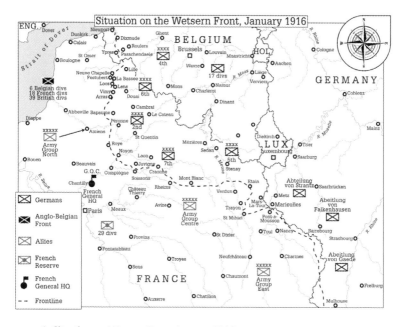

1. *Situation on Western Front, January 1916.*

or even 'place of execution'. In rough outline, Gericht involved drawing the French into a battle of attrition around Verdun, dealing it a crippling blow in its already weakened state. With France brought to its knees, Falkenhayn envisaged, the British would lose a supporting strut and its motivation to prosecute a terribly costly war on French soil. Falkenhayn knew that the forthcoming battle would also be costly in terms of the lives of his own men, but he believed that the final equations of cost would work out in Germany's favour. How wrong he would be.

It should be noted that there is a theoretical question mark over whether Falkenhayn originally planned Gericht as a

MEMORANDUM LAID BEFORE THE SECOND ALLIED MILITARY CONFERENCE AT CHANTILLY, 6 DECEMBER 1915

After the comparative failure of the operations against France and Russia, Germany, covered in the West by her main Armies and a powerful defensive system, and on the Russian front by similar dispositions of less strength, is employing in the East such forces as she still has at her disposal. The aims of the enemy in this new phase of the war are easy to understand:

• To husband his resources in men, and by slowing down the process of attrition, to be in a condition to continue the struggle indefinitely: a policy made possible by the intervention of new allies, and by the intensive employment of those he already possesses.
• In attracting its forces to secondary theatres by threats at particularly vulnerable points, to decentralise the efforts of the Coalition.
• To pursue the realisation of the German imperial idea contained in the phrase 'Drang nach Osten' so as to increase his world prestige, raise the morale of his own people, and acquire so strong a position in the East that, whatever the issue of the struggle, he could not be forced to surrender it.

pure battle of attrition. Certainly, the Crown Prince and many other commanders on the battlefront were not aware of the attrition principle. Such was, however, logically necessary to the development of the battle. By making a limited attack on the front, Falkenhayn could draw French forces into the maelstrom, but by giving his commanders clear and very achievable objectives he risked the campaign ending before attrition had taken effect. Nonetheless, many commanders and soldiers might

2. Poilus *returning to their billets after a spell on the frontline on the Western Front. (*The War Budget, *23 March 1916)*

have baulked at the idea of being used simply in some ghastly equation of death, so Falkenhayn's cautious distribution of his intentions is understandable.

THE ARMIES

The armies that composed the fighting forces at Verdun in 1916 were in many ways much changed from those that had entered the war so enthusiastically in 1914. Of course, new, fervent recruits were fed into the grinding mill of the Western Front with each passing year, but the naïveté of those first months of the war was emphatically gone. The true horror of modern weaponry was no longer a mystery, and tactics had changed accordingly – the key objectives generally became sheer survival and inflicting wearying losses on the opposing side, rather than grab for personal glory through risky action. The terrifying level of casualties, recruitment needs, plus new issues of command-and-control over vast battlefields, had also imposed organisational changes on most armies, as they attempted to find the most efficient structures for logistical and combat requirements. Yet even by 1916, there was still much learning to do. Some army commanders struggled to shake off the old ways of war, believing that sheer élan and martial spirit could triumph over bullet and shell. For both the French and the Germans, the Battle of Verdun would be a conclusive demonstration of the fallacy of this idea.

The Commanders

French commanders

At the top of the hierarchical tree of French commanders was Gen. Joseph Joffre. He had taken the position of commander-in-chief of French forces in 1911, following a military career that began in the 1870s. Judicious management of his political position – he was a good republican – as much as varied colonial experience ensured his rise up through the ranks to a position of ultimate military power. And yet, in many ways he was an unlikely candidate for the job. He was a 64-year-old man who ruthlessly insisted on a daily routine moulded around his appetites and energies – particularly regarding food and sleep. He was a man who bathed in favourable publicity, but could shrug off criticism and worry (he often restored his spirits via an epic meal). Joffre was celebrated as the saviour of France for his role in the Battle of the Marne, but by all accounts he was neither a natural nor inspirational leader of men.

*3. The defender of Verdun: General Pétain, with President Poincaré and General Joffre. (*The Illustrated War News, *15 March 1916)*

He diligently stayed away from danger and frontlines, meaning that he became an extremely distant figure to the millions of men under his command. Apart from one or two glimmers of empathy, he also appeared to feel little for the soldiers who died in their hundreds of thousands. Yet he was focused and imperturbable (unless his lunch or dinner was served late), and he managed to cope with the poisonous back-biting atmosphere that prevailed at general headquarters. An ambiguous figure, Joffre's contribution to the outcome of the war remains hotly argued.

Commander of Army Group Centre (from 30 April 1916 at least) – the army group responsible for Verdun – was Gen. Henri-Philippe Pétain. Pétain is forever etched in historical memory as the arch collaborator of the Vichy regime during the Second World War, which has clouded the lofty respect that he attained during the First World War. Unlike Joffre, Pétain radiated physical stature and authority – a fact that fostered an amorous private life – but he was a serious military officer. His progression up the ranks had been slow, and he had developed a passionate dislike of

4. Henri-Phillippe Pétain. (Wikimedia Commons)

politicians and of the intrigues of court. Through diligent studies of recent conflicts, Pétain advocated defensive firepower as the future of warfare, and in so doing put himself at odds with many of the more offensively minded generals (see the 'Tactics' section below). And although Pétain was not shy about putting soldiers' lives on the line, he also possessed a genuine understanding of and attention to the needs of the lowest ranks, especially in terms of basic logistics. He was known to visit the wounded in hospital, and he was doubtless respected by the men who fought at Verdun.

Before his army group command, Pétain was commander of the French Second Army, which passed to become the command of Gen. Robert Nivelle. Fifty-eight years old at the Battle of Verdun, Nivelle's promotion during the war years had been rapid, not only by virtue of his aggressive and bold leadership of men in combat, but also on account of his skill at handling politicians. Overarching self-confidence was both Nivelle's core strength and, ultimately, critical weakness. His steely belief in offensive spirit could make him disdainful of casualties, but his eloquence and assuring personality would convince his listeners that all was well.

Two other characters that deserve a special mention for their role at Verdun are Gen. Charles Mangin and one Major d'Alenson. The latter was Nivelle's chief of staff, and this badly dressed, physically drawn man (he was actually suffering from terminal consumption) formed a gaunt contrast to Nivelle's magnetic presence. D'Alenson appears to have been possessed by the desire to see a French victory before mortality caught up with him, and thus he was a driving presence behind Nivelle's offensive action later in the Verdun campaign, and in subsequent years.

In brutal contrast to d'Alenson, Mangin was intimidatingly physical. He was a true fighting soldier, wounded three times during his colonial service, and he took further wounds during the First World War, demonstrating a near reckless disregard for his own safety. Unfortunately, this disregard seems to have extended to the men under his command. At the beginning of the Verdun battle, Mangin was the commander of the 5th Division, but he also became Nivelle's right-hand executive officer, a man known for getting things done. He appears to have been uncaring about the slaughter at the frontline, projecting his lack of fear of death onto thousands of other servicemen. He was certainly a technically skilled officer, with a real eye for the crucial details of operational planning, but he came to be labelled as the 'butcher of Verdun' by his own countrymen. He probably couldn't have cared less.

German commanders

The two figures who stand out in terms of the German leadership are Gen. Falkenhayn, Chief of the Imperial General Staff, and the commander of the Fifth Army, Crown Prince Wilhelm, the Kaiser's son. Falkenhayn's promotion to chief of staff had been nothing short of meteoric, a fact that alongside his aristocratic origins bred arrogance and a rather blind conviction that he was always right. He had a sound grasp of military matters and could be ruthless in prosecuting his goals (both with his staff and with the lives of his men), but he could also be prey to indecision and caution, which as Horne has said often 'turned his successes into half-successes'.

Falkenhayn's burden was both strategic and political in nature. He was forever at loggerheads with Field Marshal (FM) Paul von Hindenburg, the commander-in-chief of German forces on the Eastern Front, and Hindenberg's chief of staff, Erich von Ludendorff. Both Hindenburg and Ludendorff were offensively minded proponents of focusing on the Eastern Front, while Falkenhayn was of defensive orientation and committed to a Western Front strategy. Falkenhayn fought this interminable political struggle until Hindenburg won in August 1916 when he replaced Falkenhayn as chief of staff. Falkenhayn subsequently became Hindenburg's quartermaster general, although he retained an integral relationship to the continuing Verdun campaign.

5. Erich von Falkenhayn. (Wikimedia Commons)

Crown Prince Wilhelm was a very different animal to many of the commanders described above. He was a man of contrasts. On the one hand he loved the partying and socialising of most young princes, projecting something of a playboy lifestyle that frequently brought him into trouble with his father. He also longed for military glory, but this did not mean that he was a shallow commander of the Fifth Army, which he led at Verdun at the age of just 34. Although regarded by many of his peers (with some justification) as a military amateur, he grew to have a prescient sense of strategic developments, a vision that he would demonstrate at Verdun. However, the bloodshed of Verdun was frequently laid at his feet, earning him the nickname 'the laughing murderer of Verdun'. Unlike the Teflon-coated Mangin, Wilhelm was deeply hurt by this title, but went on to army group command status in the last two years of the war.

The Soldiers

French forces

For those used to a British-oriented perspective on the First World War, it is sobering to realise how much the manpower contribution of France dwarfed that of the UK. At the outbreak of war in August 1914, the British Expeditionary Force (BEF) was able to field eight infantry divisions and two cavalry divisions, whereas the French Army – which had mobilised 2.9 million men during the summer of 1914, in expectation of war – mustered ninety-six infantry divisions and ten cavalry. Of course, Britain quickly implemented a truly enormous recruitment drive, so that by the end of the war it could draw on a total of sixty-nine infantry and five cavalry divisions. Yet even then, the French commitment was far greater – 221 infantry and six cavalry divisions. Whereas the UK mobilised a total of 5.7 million men for war service between 1914 and 1918, the French fielded 8.66 million, a vast escalation from a peacetime army of just 700,000 men.

As with most European armies, the French Army was organised by a system of armies, corps, divisions, brigades, regiments, battalions and companies. The infantry division remained the heart of the French Army's structure, and at the beginning of the war it was organised along the lines of two brigades, each of two regiments, plus a field artillery regiment (three artillery groups, each of three batteries), plus various support units, including a machine-gun section, engineer company and train squadron. Some divisions would also have an attached *Chasseur à pied* light infantry battalion, which specialised in mobile skirmishing and offensive tactics.

This structure would change significantly throughout the war as manpower losses bit into the reserves of French youth. From late 1916, even as the Battle of Verdun rumbled on, the French

Army began to reorganise its line infantry divisions along a three-regiment basis, without the intervening brigade structure. A more significant change, however, had taken place in divisional artillery. The decisive importance of artillery in the First World War is suggested by the fact that, at the beginning of the conflict, gunners constituted 20 per cent of the entire French Army, but by the end of the war that figure had increased to 38 per cent. (During the same period, the percentage of infantry had dropped from 60 per cent to 45 per cent.) The new 1916 infantry division's artillery regiment therefore included three field artillery batteries (each with four x 75mm guns), a field howitzer battery (four x 155mm howitzers), plus a trench artillery platoon, a trench artillery battery and a mortar company. Together these units delivered a major increase in the firepower of the French infantry division, as the Germans opposite would doubtless have vouched for. The French had always prided themselves on their artillery skills

*6. French cavalry, part of the forces in reserve behind Verdun, conduct an attack exercise in 1916. (*The Illustrated War News, *29 March 1916)*

(Napoleon Bonaparte was one prestigious historical artilleryman), but the increasing integration of artillery into strategic and tactical manoeuvres during the First World War placed such skills at the forefront. In terms of their organisation, it should be noted that the groups that made up a divisional artillery regiment tended to be drawn from different regiments, rather than represent a single unified regiment. The divisional regiment therefore acted as an administrative body, overseeing the various groups and batteries under its authority. The engineer aspect of the division had also become more central to operations; while the engineers of 1914 mainly focused upon telephone, telegraph, field park and bridging duties, the division of 1916 also included mining companies and dedicated signals sections.

The French infantry, artillery and engineers presented the work-a-day face of warfare in the early twentieth century, while the French cavalry kept one nostalgic and spirited foot firmly in the past. As in earlier history, the cavalry were there as exploitation forces, designed to surge through gaps created in the enemy ranks and push through into the rear areas beyond, hopefully precipitating a decisive turn in the battle or even the campaign.

The seventy-nine French cavalry units at the beginning of the war had titles that would have been familiar back in Napoleon's day – cuirassiers, dragoons, chasseurs à cheval and hussars. The experience of war on the Western Front certainly changed the tactical nature of the French cavalry, as it did amongst the cavalry of all sides. The argument that horse-mounted cavalry were redundant in the age of the machine-gun has been shown, by careful analysis, to be false, but there was certainly no doubting that firepower had made cavalry extremely vulnerable if deployed in unsupported frontal assaults. Furthermore, the very lack of flanks on the Western Front – the trenches formed a near continuous line – meant that there were few opportunities for outflanking of the enemy, previously one of the key roles of the cavalry. For such reasons, cavalry were often used as a mobile form

FRENCH CAVALRY

William Pressey, a British artilleryman, describes a French cavalry charge near Amiens on 26 March 1918:

Coming towards us were a troop of French cavalry. I should say a hundred and fifty or two hundred strong. Gosh, but they looked splendid. I think word must have got to them about the German cavalry harassing us and they had come to put a stop to that. They could never have been told about the machine guns. They laughed and waved their lances at us. We slowed down as they trotted briskly past, and everyone was looking back at them.

Before reaching the top of the hill they opened out to about six feet between each horse and in a straight line. We hardly breathed. Over the top of the hill they charged, lances at the ready. There was not a sound from us. Then, only a few seconds after they disappeared, the hellish noise of machine guns broke out. We just looked at each other. The only words I heard spoken were 'Bloody hell...' That's what it must have been over the hill, for not one man came back. Several of the horses did, and trotted beside us, and were collected at our next stopping place.

Carey, *Eyewitness to* History, p.484

of infantry, using their horses to get them into key positions on the battlefield before dismounting to fight.

Humble origins

The individual French soldier was typically drawn into the armed forces by a process of conscription. National military service was compulsory for all 20-year-old eligible males even before the start of the war, although a ballot system and multiple exemptions ensured that plenty of men avoided donning a uniform in peacetime years. The period of military service was (from 1912) three years, but after their national service a man had to remain on

7. Moroccan Tirailleurs *returned from the frontline trenches to rest. (*The Illustrated War News*, 15 March 1916)*

the reserve list for eleven years, and thereafter the territorials for a further seven years, and then the territorial reserves for another seven years, with the prospect of being called up should war break out. It was this reservoir of reservists that enabled the French to mobilise 1.1 million soldiers at the beginning of the war. Another resource on which the French could draw was the manpower of its colonies, particularly those in Africa, which were also subject to conscription. The yields for French service were substantial – France's African colonies provided 343,000 men during the war, while Indochina gave another 100,000 men. The soldiers of Verdun were mainly of indigenous French origin, but they were a mixed bag of veteran soldiers, typically in their 20s and 30s, plus ageing reservists and youthful new recruits, all adjusting to the grim realities of existence on the Western Front.

General life in the French Army, particularly during the war, was an arduous experience. Pay and conditions were poor, and the horrific bloodletting in 1914–16 bred a certain antagonism between the mass of soldiery and the high command, expressed most publicly in a series of mutinies in 1917. Nevertheless, the French soldier was capable of granite-like endurance and tenacity in both the offence and defence, and he was a respected foe amongst his German opponents. One of the biggest changes was a gradually devolving emphasis on the small unit as key to French Army tactics. Historian of Verdun William Martin has noted that:

> By the end of the First World War the battalion was no longer the manoeuvre unit. Nor was the company. It was the platoon, itself an 'all-arms' formation that included four discrete elements: machine-guns, rifle-grenades, light mortars, hand grenades – as well as rifles. Infantrymen fought in squads of eight to ten men, using 'fire and manoeuvre tactics whereby some squads advanced by short rushes while others provided covering fire.

> William Martin, *Verdun 1916: 'They Shall Not Pass'*,
> pp.17–18

The French Army of 1916 was in the middle of this transition. Straddling traditionalism and innovation, it was, as we shall see, a force of men caught in the midst of titanic forces affecting the very nature of warfare itself. Yet much about their life in the trenches remained primitive in nature. Conditions on the frontline were almost invariably appalling. There appears to have been a neglectful attitude towards hygiene and sanitation amongst many French units at this time, a fact commented upon by many British observers. Filth, lice and their accompanying diseases seemed to have been tolerated to a far greater degree by the French *poilu* (literally 'hairy one', an informal term for the French infantryman in the First World War) than by many other nations, probably on account of the very rural nature of much of France. Food was the one recompense. In the first months of the war the standards of cuisine for the French soldier were generally very high, but during 1915 the demands of increased manpower and problems with supplying adequate cooking facilities meant that rations devolved

The French Soldier at Verdun

The infantry represented by far the largest element of the French Army, and roughly 80 per cent of the infantry was composed of men from rural backgrounds. The infantry regiments had a local identity, so the men in each regiment might serve alongside friends from their local town or village. In terms of the journey from recruitment office to the frontline, the soldier would pass through training companies, then rear-area battalions that helped him adjust to life near the front, while also providing training in specialist skills (such as signaller or machine-gunner). From here the recruit would then journey up to the frontline, to join a combat regiment. At the opening of the Verdun offensive in February 1916, the typical French soldier was clad in the horizon blue tunic and trousers, with an outer wrapping of the Modéle (Mle) 1914/15 greatcoat and head protection courtesy of the Mle 1915 Adrian pattern steel helmet. His personal world was carried in the Mle 1893/1914 knapsack, the contents of which revealed every soldier's priority at the frontline. Apart from a few non-essential items from home, generally kept to a minimum for reasons of weight saving, much of the pack's contents was devoted to food.

Typical contents might include tins of beef, packets of biscuits, a bag of coffee, and salt and sugar, plus requisite cooking and eating utensils, including metal bowls and a coffee grinder (to each section). Popular Anglo-centric history has not been kind to the French soldier, yet a closer look shows an enormous capacity for both bravery and resilience.

8. French soldier, 1916. (The Illustrated War News, 19 April 1916)

into the typically bland compositions of poor-quality meats and soft vegetables.

None of this helped morale, of course, nor did it foster good relationships between the officers and men. Historians of the French Army of the First World War have often commented upon the fact that, despite its republican and revolutionary past, the French military had a rigorously enforced hierarchy, with the officers occupying a distant and often disdainful strata above the other ranks. To be fair, the officer class had suffered appalling percentages of losses in 1914 and 1915 (Alistair Horne notes that 50 per cent of regular cadre officers were lost during these two years), and so those who were left were doubtless aware of how distinct they were. The losses amongst the officers often resulted in the rapid promotion of senior NCOs to officer status, although these men seem to have been scarcely more affable to the lower ranks than those who had been commissioned as their first step in a military career. The separation between officers and men, temporarily closed to some degree during battle, was doubtless a contributing factor in the major mutinies amongst the French Army in 1917, following the disastrous Nivelle Offensive for which the *poilus* bled another river of blood.

German forces

Looking across the battlefield, the German Army of 1916 had also ridden the steep learning curve of modern warfare, and had equally experienced grotesque losses on both the Western and the Eastern Fronts. It was, nevertheless, a thoroughly professional organisation, composed at the outbreak of war by four armies – those of the kingdoms of Prussia, Bavaria, Saxony and Württemberg – and centred on the Kaiser, the head of state, commander-in-chief and an enthusiast for all things military.

At the beginning of the war, the German Army demonstrated a formidable skill in mobilisation – utilising Germany's major railway network (partly developed under military direction), 1.7 million German soldiers were in the field at the outset of the war, the manpower mobilising four times faster than it had during the Franco-Prussian War. Some 113 infantry divisions and eleven cavalry divisions swung into action. The structure of the infantry divisions bore some similarities to that of the French Army, and also likewise underwent reorganisation during the first two years of the war. In 1914 the infantry division contained two core infantry brigades, each of two infantry regiments of three battalions. An artillery headquarters presided over a field artillery regiment, in turn composed of two field gun detachments (each of three batteries of four x 77mm guns) and a field howitzer detachment (three batteries of four x 105mm howitzers). A cavalry squadron provided the division with its rapid-manoeuvre element.

From the spring of 1915, new German infantry divisions were formed with just a single infantry brigade, but of three regiments rather than two. Yet the most significant change to the German division was in terms of its allocations of firepower. Before the autumn of 1916, each regiment was allocated a machine-gun company, initially of six heavy machine-guns. The weapon strength of this company was progressively increased to twelve machine-guns, then each battalion received its own machine-gun company, each of which swelled from four guns to twelve by the end of the war. From the autumn of 1916 the divisions on the Western Front also tended to acquire a separate machine-gun detachment three companies strong, each with twelve machine-guns. The effect was essentially a 600 per cent increase in automatic firepower within the German infantry division, illustrating how significant the machine-gun was within German defensive strategy.

Germany's cavalry traditions were not as strong as those of France, and the German Army's relationship to its eleven cavalry divisions reflected an emergent scepticism about the role of this arm. A cavalry division consisted of three brigades, each of three regiments, each of four squadrons, plus a Jäger battalion and various artillery, signals, mortar and pioneer detachments. Germany's largely defensive outlook, plus the problems of finding enough suitable mounts for the cavalry troops, meant that no less than seven of the eleven cavalry divisions were disbanded from October 1916, the regiments being turned into dismounted units known as Cavalry Marksmen Commands.

The German Army was manned by three different types of soldier: active (regular), reservist and *Landwehr* or *Landsturm*. The last two on this list were territorial and second-line reservists, and their quality could not be guaranteed. Thus it should be remembered that not all German soldiers were equivalent to the professional assault troops that emerged later in the war. Nonetheless, the regular and component reservist battalions were indeed capable warriors, not least because of the nature of German command relationships. The German Army had a very centralised command system, trickling down from the Kaiser and the General Staff at the very top to the humble *Soldat* at the very bottom. Where the Germans did excel, however, was in an excellent and numerous NCO strata. (The German units had three times as many NCOs compared to their British equivalents.) There were undoubted problems with this system, and it could make battlefield command a complex business at times, yet it also made the smaller German units – such as the *Gruppe* (Group; eight to nine men) or *Korporalschaften* (Section; sixteen to eighteen men) – more self-reliant, and less prone to collapse once an officer had been killed, wounded or otherwise taken out of the equation.

Although the Germans, like all other soldiers on the Western Front, suffered from the physical conditions of trench life, they tended to demonstrate far higher standards of field engineering than the French. Dug-outs and bunkers were constructed with admirable attention to both resilience and comfort. Concrete emplacements were built that ran many metres below the ground, where they were impervious to shellfire above and also provided secure accommodation to dozens, sometimes

The German Soldier at Verdun

Germany's manpower was familiar with military service even before the war. Everyone between the ages of 17 and 45 was eligible for this service, joining the *Landsturm* (Home Guard) at the age of 17 and the regular army from the age of 20. Regular army service would last for two or, for cavalry and artillery, three years, after which the man would be passed on to the reserve forces, which formed a large part of the army that mobilised in 1914. The quality of the individual German soldier, as in all armies, could vary distinctly between units. Some of the reserve units could be shaky in action, and hence were consigned to relatively quiet sectors, while combat-experienced regular divisions constituted some of the best formations on the entire front. During the Battle of Verdun, a further distinction was found between the general infantryman and the elite *Stosstruppen* (Stormtroopers – see 'Tactics' section on pp.61–63). The latter were amongst the first German troops to receive the new *Stahlhelm* (steel helmet) in early 1916, and in action they carried extra amounts of grenades and small-arms ammunition. They even had leather patches sewn onto their uniforms over the knees and elbows, to protect their joints while crawling. When not on the offensive, the *Stosstruppen* lived the life of every other German soldier. Rations were a perennial problem: the daily ration of 1914 featured 750g (26oz) of bread or 400–500g (14–18oz) of biscuit, plus 375g (13oz) of fresh meat and various vegetables. By the middle of the Verdun battle, however, the meat ration alone had slumped to 200g (7oz), and other rations were hard pressed – there were few frontline German soldiers carrying excess weight in 1916.

9. German soldier, 1916. (Author's collection)

hundreds, of men. Such positions were often fully equipped with electricity, furniture, drainage systems and other modern features, and they are doubtless part of the reason the Germans were able to demonstrate such defensive fortitude.

The Kit

The armies of the First World War were both the beneficiaries and the victims of a remarkable revolution in firepower that had occurred the previous century. The advent of breech-loading, bolt-action and automatic small arms, firing unitary cartridges, had made the days of muzzle-loading, single-shot weapons a distant memory, and had given the individual soldier the means to generate significant personal firepower. A bolt-action, magazine-fed rifle could fire up to fifteen aimed shots per minute in trained hands, while a single Maxim machine-gun could fire up to 450rpm (rounds per minute). In the field of infantry warfare, attrition was now possible on an industrial scale.

The primary weapon for the soldiers of all sides was the bolt-action rifle. For the French this meant either the 8mm Mle 1886 Lebel or one of several types of Berthier rifle, named after the man who had headed the design committee behind the rifle, André Berthier. The Lebel was the French Army's first magazine-fed rifle, and had an eight-round, under-barrel magazine. The 8 x 50R cartridge it fired was powerful enough, but the length of the weapon (1,295mm or 51in), plus the nature of the magazine design (the rifle's centre of gravity altered every time the rifle reloaded), meant that it was not a particularly accurate weapon over distance, nor was it convenient in the close-quarters melee of a trench fight. Nevertheless, it was the personal weapon of the bulk of French infantry and would remain in action throughout the next world war.

The Berthier rifle was designed when the French ordnance authorities began to make unfavourable comparisons between the Lebel and the competing Mauser and Mannlicher rifles from Germany. A carbine that married the Lebel's bolt action with an integral box magazine similar to that of the German Mannlicher was produced – the Mle 1890 – and modified versions appeared at intervals over the next two decades, including rifle-length versions from 1902. The Berthiers were actually much better suited to trench warfare than the Lebel rifle, being more robust and better at delivering aimed fire over practical combat ranges. The major deficiency of the Berthier was its limited ammunition capacity – just three rounds – so in 1916 a modified version was issued that increased the magazine size to hold five rounds. Both the Lebel and the Berthier could be fitted with lengthy knife bayonets, which, although intended for spirited bayonet charges, tended to have more applications in simple daily chores, such as opening ration packets.

The Germans had a single model of the bolt-action rifle to guide them through the war – the 7.92mm M1898 (Gewehr 98). Slightly shorter than the Lebel and Berthier rifle at 1,255mm (49.4in), and weighing 4.14kg (9lb), the Gewehr 98 was built around the excellent Mauser bolt-action rifle, a model of reliability even amidst the dirt and detritus of trench conditions (although the action was somewhat slower to operate than many Allied rifles). It had a five-round integral box magazine, which was loaded through the opened action via a stripper clip, and when fitted with a basic telescopic sight it could take accurate shots well beyond 600m (656yd). Indeed, many an Allied soldier met his end by revealing his head for just a fraction of a second above a trench parapet, thereby attracting the accurate attentions of German snipers. In battle the Mauser was utterly dependable, and its contribution to German firepower on the Western Front cannot be underestimated.

Despite the power of the rifle, the fact remained that the heart of battalion firepower came from its machine-guns. The French were not entirely well served in this regard. The best of their machine-guns was the Hotchkiss gun, which first entered service in 1897 and went through several ostensibly improved versions by the beginning of the war. (The principal First World War version was the Mle 1914.) The Hotchkiss was a gas-operated weapon and chambered for the 8mm Lebel rifle cartridge. It was a heavy (23.58kg/51lb) weapon whose largely sound operating mechanism was let down by a poor ammunition feed system – rigid twenty-four- or thirty-round metallic strips which were awkward to feed in and were easily damaged in frontline use. (Articulated belts were introduced in 1917.) Unlike the water-cooled heavy machine-guns used by many contemporary armies, the Hotchkiss was air-cooled. The setup had the advantage of making the total weapon package lighter to transport around the battlefield, but the gunner also had to be careful to control his fire – sustained fire could quickly lead to barrel overheating and malfunctions.

The Hotchkiss was not perfect, but it was nearing mechanical heaven when compared to some of the shockingly poor alternatives within the French arsenals. Pre-war attempts to improve on the Hotchkiss resulted in making the undeniably worse 8mm Puteaux Mle 1905, and its successor the 8mm Saint-Etienne Mle 1907. Both were over-complex and mechanically unreliable, especially in warfare conditions, and so they had limited use on the Western Front. The 8mm Chauchat Mle 1915, however, actually received widespread distribution, despite it being widely regarded as one of the worst machine-guns ever made. Almost nothing about its design is praiseworthy. Fed from a poorly designed, curved twenty-round magazine, the Chauchat offered the soldier little but violent recoil, regular malfunctions, constant field stripping and inaccuracy. It must have been a soul-sinking task to trust one's survivability to such a firearm.

The Germans at Verdun would have put their trust in a far superior brand of machine-gun, the 7.92mm Maxim MG08. As the name suggests, this weapon was essentially a tweaked and improved version of Hiram Maxim's original machine-gun. It was recoil-operated, water-cooled (meaning it could handle sustained fire with a limited risk of overheating) and built to last. Set up on its hefty bipod, the MG08 could rattle out fire at a cyclical rate of 300–450rpm, hour after hour, its 7.92 x 57mm Mauser rifle rounds killing at ranges of well over 1,500m (1,640yd). The main downside to the MG08, however, was its sheer weight. The empty gun alone weighed 26.4kg (58lb), but with its comprehensive Schlitten 08 sled carriage, plus spare parts, the total kit weighed 62kg (136lb), to be carried alongside ammunition by a crew of four. The Germans made a brave attempt to convert the MG08 into a light machine-gun (LMG) by fitting the basic gun with a pistol grip, shoulder stock and light bipod. The result was lighter but still too heavy for a light machine-gun; the MG08/15, as it was known, nevertheless made an important contribution to German firepower on the Western Front, and remained superior to many of the French weapons.

The infantry on both sides were equipped with a selection of other personal weapons, both improvised and issue. A wide variety of grenades was used: the proliferation of types was

*10. On a 'rocking frame' mount: A single-barrelled 'revolver-cannon' employed by the French at Verdun. (*The Illustrated War News, *5 April 1916)*

11. A French soldier prepares to throw a grenade, while his comrade prepares the fuse of another. (The Illustrated War News, 5 April 1916)

particularly excessive in the French Army, and ranged from improvised weapons consisting of demolition charges tied to sticks, through to advanced 'pineapple' type fragmentation grenades such as the *Grenade Fusante nr1*, which became the most common French grenade in use from early 1916. The Germans used four principal types: the *Stielhandgranate* (stick hand grenade), the *Diskushandgranate* (disc hand grenade), *Eierhandgranate* (egg hand grenade) and *Kugelhandgranate* (ball hand grenade), with the grenade name indicative of its format.

FLAMETHROWERS

The Germans were amongst the first to adopt man-portable flamethrowers for their infantry units, deploying them on the battlefield from 1915. The small *Kleinflammenwerfer*, for example, could throw out a jet of flame to a distance of about 6m (20ft), useful for close-quarters work against trench systems. The larger *Grossflammenwerfer* could launch its flame to three times that distance, and was operated by two men – one to carry the fuel/ gas tanks, and the other to wield the fire lance.

Grenades were extremely useful tools in the context of trench warfare, with dedicated bomber soldiers used to clear trench sections systematically. If the combat moved to close-quarters, then pistols (largely for officers) became more practical. The standard French pistol was the Mle 1892, an underpowered 8mm six-shot revolver that featured a side-opening chamber. The Germans had the excellent and modern Parabellum Model 1908 Luger, a semi-automatic 9mm gun that worked off an eight-round detachable box magazine in the grip. The Luger's quick reloading capability and large (for the time) magazine capacity made it a business-like tool in a trench scrap. Beyond firearms, both sides always had recourse to lengthy, torso-skewering bayonets, or a nightmarish selection of improvised clubs, knives, sharpened spades and other crude devices.

A study of the weapons used by the French and Germans at Verdun would not be complete without a brief look at the nature of each side's artillery. The crucial importance of artillery to the conflict has already been noted, and the types of artillery firepower available to each side affected the very nature of the clash at Verdun. The French relied primarily on the Canon de 75 Mle 1897, or variants thereof, which was a quick-firing 75mm weapon and one of the great artillery pieces of the

12. Tracking a 6in shell in flight: A French gunner following with his eye a long-range shot. (The Illustrated War News, 22 March 1916)

nineteenth and twentieth centuries. It could fire at a sustained rate of 15rpm, and its advanced gas and oil recoil mechanism meant it could maintain its accuracy even at full rate of fire. The 75mm was, however, a true field gun, light and easy to deploy but with a rather flat trajectory, which made it unsuited to returning the pounding long-range bombardments that the Germans delivered at Verdun. Heavier firepower was available in the form of larger guns such as the Canon de 105 Mle 1913 Schneider, which had a range out to 12km (7.5 miles) – the 75mm's maximum range was just under 7km (4.3 miles) – but in total the 75mm fired 75 per cent of all French shells at Verdun.

The German artillery, brought to bear with such devastating effect at Verdun, included a far higher percentage of earth-shaking siege guns. These weapons were of punishing calibres, ranging from 150mm to 305mm and even 420mm (the legendary 'Big Bertha' guns), and were capable of reducing even the most stubborn of defences to rubble. These two very different concepts of artillery would be tested in battle throughout 1916.

Uniforms

As in the case of weaponry, the First World War was also a conflict that saw a significant change in the nature of uniforms. This was especially the case with the French Army. The French had begun the war wearing a uniform that was not only impractical, but actively dangerous. The basic uniform featured a blue tunic, dark-blue greatcoat, bright-red trousers (tucked into leather boots or puttees) and a traditional red *kepi* cloth cap. The colourful combination was an enemy marksmen's dream, and was a contributing factor to the appalling losses amongst the French infantry during 1914–15. The wearying influx of head casualties into aid stations, and fatal head wounds on the frontline (13.3 per cent of all wounds were head wounds), also revealed that the *kepi* provided a skull with no protection against bullet or shell fragment.

The year 1915 brought some necessary and welcome changes. Most significant was the introduction of a new uniform made from *horizon bleu* (horizon blue) cloth; gone were the conspicuous red trousers. This was not camouflage, but it definitely made the French soldier stand out less on a drab battlefield. Another major change was the introduction of the Mle 1915 Adrian pattern steel helmet from September 1915. This distinctive helmet, with its high crown and prominent brim, was not the last word in head protection; it was made from mild steel, which was both heavy for the wearer yet had limited protective properties. But compared to the *kepi* it was an important step forward, and it consequently brought about a significant reduction in the volume of head injuries.

The German forces also began the war with an impractical form of headgear – the M1895 Pickelhaube, made from boiled leather and surmounted by a prominent decorative metal spike. This relic of Germany's imperial past was finally replaced in 1916 by the M1916 Stahlhelm (steel helmet), a substantial metal helmet that offered ballistic protection to both the skull and the back of the neck, and whose basic shape would go on to inform the helmets worn by the German Army in the Second World War.

German Army uniforms also evolved during the first years of the war, but the soldier of 1914 was already clad in a fairly utilitarian field-grey uniform and matching M1907 greatcoat. The uniform was subsequently adapted to frontline life, but also to the hard economic realities of wartime mass production. The design was simplified and materials frequently cheapened. Like all soldiers on the Western Front at this time, the German infantryman who had spent a few months at the front had a uniform with all the colour and grace of old dish cloths.

13. *The* Poilu's *cup of tea* a l'anglaise *at the front. (*The Illustrated War News, *5 April 1916)*

FRENCH ARMY FASHION

Henry Hamilton Fyfe, a journalist with the *Daily Mail*, witnessed the appearance of the French soldier in the first months of the war:

The whole country swarmed already with soldiers. Most of them were middle-aged, none of their uniforms fitted. They wore the absurd red trousers below the blue coat which had been in fashion since Napoleon's time. I recall a conversation with a French journalist who assured me that the army would lose all spirit if its red trousers were taken away. He would not listen to me when I said the uniform would have to be altered, as the British red coats were changed to khaki in South Africa. That was the general attitude of Frenchmen.

Tactics

Verdun was a battle that saw two competing strategies clash in an epic struggle for supremacy. The tactics at the heart of each strategy were an expression not only of military thinking, but also of cultural biases at the heart of the French and the German nations.

The French Army had done much soul searching in the aftermath of its defeat during the Franco-Prussian War. The main conclusion, one that would permeate French military thinking for the next fifty years, was that the key to victory was an offensive mindset. Defensive or cautious tactics were increasingly spurned, as Alistair Horne has brilliantly conveyed:

> There was talk about the posture of attack being most suited to the national temperament… The new mood was also well-matched to the philosophy of Bergson that was now all the rage in France, with its emphasis on the élan vital. As the years

moved farther away from the actual experience of war, so the philosophy of the offensive moved ever farther from reality. At pre-war French manoeuvres, British observers with memories from the Veldt were always struck by the antipathy to going to ground. At the École de Guerre little study was made of the successes of the defence in the American Civil War, the Boer War or in the recent significant fighting in Manchuria. In fact, there was little pragmatic study of any sort…

Horne, Price of Glory, p.11

The embodiment of the offensive philosophy in the wartime years was found in Colonel (Col) de Grandmaison, Chief of the Troisième Bureau (Operations Bureau), General Staff. There were two fundamental components to de Grandmaison's philosophy. The first was that only in the assault did the French soldier find fulfilment and the French Army find victory. Although the firepower of the enemy was acknowledged, the spirit of the soldier could, in de Grandmaison's view, still triumph in the face of a wall of shot and shell. The second critical element was that ground should not be yielded to the enemy under any circumstances. In these regards, de Grandmaison's philosophy was not unlike that of Hitler in 1943–45. It placed an almost mystical sense of trust in the offensive spirit, regardless of the practical difficulties in the way. Moreover, de Grandmaison hooked large numbers of believers amongst the French high command and lower down the leadership ranks.

As always, theoretical tactical models had to adjust to the realities of war. In 1914–15, the typical French offensive was conducted in a linear fashion, with troops advancing evenly in line behind an artillery barrage, delivering suppressive small-arms fire until close enough to launch a bayonet assault. Command-and-control over this phase of the attack was limited; basically the frontline leaders were there to keep the troops moving forward en masse. The deficiencies of this tactical

14. French bayonet charge, 1916. (Author' collection)

approach became shockingly apparent very quickly. German machine-guns and artillery cut ghastly lanes through the ranks of infantry, clearly demonstrating that all the martial spirit in the world counted for nothing if a soldier was struck by a 7.92mm ball round. The French use of artillery was also poor, lacking efficient coordination with the infantry advance, and delivered limited effects due to the preponderance of 75mm guns in the arsenal, rather than the heavier guns that could smash up an entrenched defence.

Necessary changes began to take place in 1916 – 1.2 million casualties in 1914–15 carried heavy persuasion. Instead of a single massive wave of infantry, preceded by skirmishers who advanced to contact, the French now structured their attacks on the basis of three waves. The first wave consisted of assault troops armed with plentiful grenades (particularly the useful VB rifle grenade) and, for what it was worth, the Chauchat LMG, plus engineers to handle wire obstructions. Their role was to make a fast drive through to the first line of enemy trenches, capture them, then push further on. A second wave of assault infantry would follow closely on their heels, serving as a reserve to the first wave and suppressing enemy positions as needed.

The third wave of troops consolidated the gains, and finished off the last pockets of resistance.

Historian Ian Sumner has pointed out the flexibility of the French Army's tactical innovations, but also the problems:

> The first two waves might be in extended order, with four or five paces between each man, but the third and fourth could be columns of squads, to make it easier to manoeuvre quickly. Yet, all too frequently, the pace and form of attacks were ruled by a rigid timetable that left insufficient discretion to local commanders to exploit success.
>
> Ian Sumner, *French Poilu 1914–18*, p.48

The picture Sumner paints is of an army somewhere between de Grandmaison's offensive enthusiasm, and the practical fire and manoeuvre tactics that had become more established by the end of the war. It was an improvement, but limitations in command-and-control meant that French tactics would remain terribly costly for some time yet.

On the German side, we find an army more wholeheartedly exploring the potential of assault tactics on the battlefield. In 1915, looking for ways to break the deadlock on the Western Front, the German Army formed an experimental assault unit called *Sturmabteilung Kaslow* (Assault Detachment Kaslow). It tested out a more mobile brand of warfare, centred around light 37mm cannon (to suppress enemy machine-guns), speed of manoeuvre and intense concentrations of small-arms fire and bombing (grenade) tactics. The soldiers were given leeway to adapt uniforms and select kit; some even donned crude metal body armour. The initial results on the battlefield were not good, but they were promising enough to encourage development further, and they were refined by innovative officer Captain (Capt.) Willy Ernst Rohr from August 1915. Rohr invested in intensive training, focusing on speed of movement, gaining fire superiority (flamethrowers and light mortars were carried alongside plentiful LMGs), encouraging independent thinking amongst the men and gathering as much good intelligence as possible to support an operation. Deployed to Verdun in February 1916, Sturmabteilung Rohr proved its offensive capabilities in the early actions of this great battle and grew to battalion-strength formations during the rest of the year. By the time that the Battle of Verdun drew to a close, thirty German divisions included stormtrooper units.

The stormtroopers were undeniably a small, elite percentage of the overall German forces deployed at Verdun, but they reflected some general truths about the German Army. It was largely more tolerant of individual initiative at the frontline, although command-and-control issues still meant that attacks might be delivered in a rather rigid fashion. It was also psychologically accustomed to the war of movement; the war on the Eastern Front, unlike that of its Western counterpart (post-1914, at least), was one in which serious amounts of ground were both taken and lost. Yet interestingly, the German forces also developed the tactics of defensive warfare to extremely high levels, arguably better than those of their opponents. German trenches were formed, like those of the French, in a series of roughly parallel supporting lines. However, while the French would concentrate the weight of its combat soldiery (about two-thirds of each regiment) in the forward trench, the Germans opted for a lightly manned frontline, the reasoning being that this trench line would be the most heavily bombarded in an attack. (At Verdun, in fact, German frontline troops were often told to abandon their trench under bombardment, hiding out in deep underground dugouts or in nearby shellholes.) The weight of the German troop numbers was therefore kept much further back in second and third lines of trenches, creating an 'elastic defence' that could deliver a powerful counter-attack just at the point the enemy attack was running out of steam. This tactic was a key reason why, time and time again, we see Allied offensives make promising initial gains that were subsequently lost a few days into the battle.

Verdun would be a hellish test of both sides' tactics. Furthermore, it would also be a nightmarish exercise in endurance for the men at the frontline.

THE DAYS
BEFORE BATTLE

The fortress town of Verdun was, by all accounts, noticeably vulnerable in the days leading up to the beginning of the German offensive. The town itself sat ensconced behind a roughly circular protective shield of fortifications, with the most intensive groups of fortresses to the north and north-west. The concentric rings of forts worked with the rolling contours of the French countryside and were intelligently sited – the major forts sat on the crests of hills and high features – to work in a mutually supporting role, with valleys forming natural conduits in which invaders would be cut to ribbons by interlocking fire. The River Meuse bisected the fortified area. To the east of the river lay the major forts (from north to south, albeit in staggered fashion) of Douaumont, Vaux, Souville, Belleville, Tavannes, St Michel, Moulainville, Belrupt, Rozellier and Haudanville, supported by multiple gun batteries. To the west of the river, the Bois Bourrus ridge held a total of five evenly spaced forts, with four further south to protect Verdun's immediate western approaches.

Fort Douaumont, nearest the frontline of the positions, was the mightiest of the nineteen major and forty minor fortress in the region, 400m (437yd) long and protected by a steel-reinforced

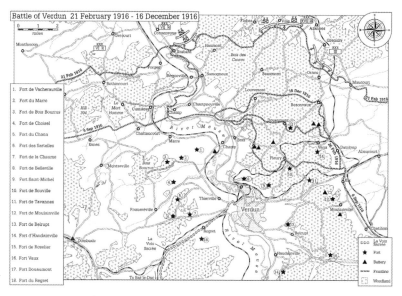

15. Battle of Verdun, 21 February 1916–16 December 1916.

concrete roof some 12m (39ft) thick. Just prior to the war, Douaumont's firepower was to be respected – a 155mm and a 75mm gun set in rotating/retractable gun turrets, four other 75mm guns in casemates, multiple machine-gun turrets and Hotchkiss cannon emplacements. As we have already noted, however, the forts around Verdun were largely emasculated during the immediate pre-war years, and in the early years of the conflict. Douaumont was no exception, and in 1915 its main armament was stripped down to just one 155mm and one 75mm gun – these were only left because they were too difficult to remove. Its garrison similarly declined to less than sixty men. Here was a lion without its teeth.

The story was repeated amongst many of the forts around Verdun. Horne notes that by October 1915 'the equivalent of forty-three heavy (plus 128,000 rounds) and eleven field-gun

16. Fort Douaumont, 1916. (Wikimedia Commons)

batteries had been removed' (Horne, *Price of Glory*, p.50). William Martin, in his book *Verdun 1916*, has judiciously observed that this policy in itself was not the true '*scandale de Verdun*' (p.25). The ability of German siege guns to smash static fortress targets had already been proven in the opening phase of the war, at places such as Anvers, Liége, Mauberge and Namur. Furthermore, the 'Russians lost vast quantities of guns when some of their forts were bypassed, surrounded and starved out' (*ibid.*). Hence it was justifiable that guns might have more utility tied to field armies than fortresses, and the French Army needed every heavy-calibre piece it could muster. Instead, Martin correctly argues that the real problem with the French was the corrosive failure of its intelligence services to detect the gathering

17. An angle of the fort against which thousands of German guns hammered in vain. (The War Budget, 20 April 1916)

storm just across the frontline, in the days before battle began. Right up the very moment when siege artillery started to smash into French positions, complacency was the order of the day amongst many of those at the top.

During the first weeks of 1916, evidence began to flow steadily towards the French that, had it been analysed seriously, would have suggested a forthcoming offensive in the region. From 17 January, when poor winter weather gave way to clearer skies, aerial photography indicated a build-up of both troops and artillery batteries in the German lines. This invaluable reconnaissance resource was nevertheless stunted by poor coordination and a general lack of personnel trained in the analysis of aerial photographs. It was also noted that there was a threefold increase in German railway movements. German deserters began to tell tales of a great impending offensive. Yet on the ground, the number of French patrols dedicated to investigating activity across the line was woefully inadequate, and the 'intercepts' of the field telephone listening posts were patchy at best, a poor example of an early form of signals intelligence. Up until early January 1916, one of France's best sources of intelligence was a network of spies, led by Louise de Bettignies, behind the German lines. In a major setback, German counter-intelligence broke the spy ring, consigning sixty agents to death or imprisonment and severing yet another avenue of vital information.

Despite the intelligence problems, there appears to have been enough information flowing from across the frontline to alert the more vigilant commanders to a gathering threat. Some of the French officers became like the mythical Cassandra, fated to predict disasters but be ignored for their pains. Close to the date of the German offensive, a Gen. Becker of XXX Corps made a report to Commandant Desoffy de Csernek et Tarko, the operations officer for Frédéric-Georges Herr, the governor of Verdun with responsibility for the defence of the entire sector. The report contained information that a German offensive at Verdun was impending, based on the evidence of aerial photographs and intelligence gleaned from deserters. Tarko was nothing short of dismissive, arguing that unless the German frontline was in visible proximity (about 800m/874yd separated the German and French frontlines) then he didn't accede to

18. French defence work representative of many miles of the French front. (The Illustrated War News, 15 March 1916)

a threat. Herr himself also didn't buy into the reports, but did push for an increase in resources to strengthen his defences. In fact, troop numbers at Verdun were reduced in late 1915 and early 1916, thousands of men being redeployed to serve in the lively Champagne sector. Many of those who remained were actually employed making partial improvements to the French defences west of the Meuse – i.e. behind Verdun – and only when it was too late were they sent to concentrate their efforts on the crucial eastern defences. By this time, German artillery pieces were even firing the odd ranging barrage, to register their guns for the forthcoming storm. Herr pleaded with general headquarters for more men to reinforce his sector. Some did arrive – two new divisions and two new corps (VII and XXX) from 12 February – but by this time the launch hour for Operation Gericht was just days away, and the influx of troops was woefully inadequate.

Another French soldier at odds with the prevailing complacency was one Lieutenant Colonel (Lt Col) Émile Driant, commander of the 56th and 59th *Chasseurs à Pied* battalions. Driant would later become one of the towering figures of the Battle of Verdun, but in 1915 he was little more than an irritant to the French high command. Driant was a true soldier's officer, knowledgeable about both the art and reality of warfare. He took command of the Chasseurs battalions in 1915, the battalions being positioned in the wooded Bois des Caures to the north-east of Verdun. By late 1915, Driant was acutely frustrated by the lack of defensive investment in the Verdun region, which he deduced was a weak point in the French line, one that the Germans would inevitably exploit. Finding no one in the immediate command chain to listen to his point of view, Driant approached an old government friend, Paul Deschanel, president of the Chamber of Deputies, and the report in turn worked its way up through Minister of War Joseph Galliéni to Gen. Joffre himself. The content of Driant's report was emphatic:

The sledge-hammer blow will be delivered on the line Verdun-Nancy. What moral effect would be created by the capture of one of these cities! … We are doing everything, day and night, to make our front inviolable … but there is one thing about which one can do nothing; *the shortage of hands*. And it is to this that I beg you to call the attention of the Minister of Defence. If our first line is carried by massive attack, our second line is inadequate and we are not succeeding in establishing it; *lack of workers* and I add: *lack of barbed wire*.

Quoted in Horne, *Price of Glory*, p.52

If Joffre had accepted the report, the development of the Battle of Verdun could have been very different. As it was, he was furious that an upstart lieutenant colonel could bypass the regular chain of command and rock the boat. He replied vehemently, and in conclusion stated: 'To sum up, I consider nothing justifies the fear which, in the name of the Government, you express in your dispatch of December 16.'

Thus it was that just a handful of French divisions occupied the 13km (8-mile) sector that would bear the brunt of the German assault. West of the Meuse, from east to west along the frontline, these were the 72nd Division, 51st Division and 14th Division. The 132nd and 3rd Divisions occupied positions 8–16km (5–10 miles) below 14th Division. West of the river, the frontline was occupied by the 29th and 67th Divisions, while the Verdun sector reserve, to the south-west of the city, included the 37th and 48th Divisions plus various other battalions. Compared to the storm clouds darkening the skies across the frontline, these forces were a fragile defence.

German Preparations

While the French remained largely in denial, the Germans were obviously using their time for far more industrious purposes. Operation Gericht was going to be a huge action, involving three corps of the German Fifth Army for the initial push. These corps were VII, XVIII and III, the first two facing the unfortunate 72nd Division while III Corps would attack the 51st Division. To the west of the Meuse was VI Corps, while V and XV Corps were positioned to the east in reserve.

The gathering of men and materiel was enormous – 140,000 troops for the attack, plus 2.7 million artillery shells. (Other materiel brought up to the frontline included a million sandbags.) To facilitate this movement, no fewer than ten train lines were constructed, plus numerous associated stations, and thousands of vehicles and horse-drawn wagons were applied to transferring the men, weaponry and equipment from the railheads to the frontline.

However, the sheer mass of humanity, wood and metal moving to the frontline would create problems all of its own. Housing the men was an obvious quandary; many soldiers would have to march several miles to the frontline during the day, then several miles back again to their billets at night. A more interesting innovation was the construction of massive underground concrete shelters called *Stollen*, each capable of holding hundreds of men. Not only did these provide a form of temporary housing, but they helped shield large volumes of men from the prying eyes of French reconnaissance aircraft. (These were also kept away by increasing German fighter patrols over the frontline, preventing French aircraft from penetrating the rear of the lines or from dawdling too long over German positions.) Unfortunately, the *Stollen* flooded easily, and in the heavy winter rains they became water-logged, miserable places in which to hunker down for the night.

Falkenhayn's plan for Verdun relied to an unprecedented extent on massive, complex and crushing artillery fire across the front. More than 1,400 artillery pieces were pushed forward in readiness, including 305mm and 420mm howitzers and even three 380mm naval guns mounted for land use. These potent guns, plus the hundreds of field artillery pieces available, meant that the preparatory barrage would be able to range far and wide across the French sector, hitting supply lines, forts and troop concentrations well behind the initial line of attack. German artillery orders expressly stated that: 'No line is to remain unbombarded, no possibilities of supply unmolested, nowhere should the enemy feel safe.' In total, the barrage was scheduled to last for some nine hours, by which time more than a million shells would have ravaged the French positions. Once the pounding lifted, then the three frontal army corps would surge forward in the attack, pushing down from the north across a relatively narrow front and capturing as many positions as possible. Stormtroopers armed with flamethrowers and bags of grenades would be in the vanguard, punching holes into the French lines for the mass of infantry to exploit. Given Falkenhayn's attritional objective for Verdun, the long-term exposition of the battle plan was unclear. The ideal objective was

*19. After a heavy bombardment, the German soldiers attacked Verdun over devastated ground such as this. (*The War Budget, *30 March 1916)*

to advance to capture not only the key forts, but also the town of Verdun itself. Once the advance reached its natural limits the Germans would then dig in and let the French spill their blood trying to recapture the German gains.

Operation Gericht was scheduled to begin in the dark hours before dawn on 12 February 1916. The weather, however, had other ideas. On 11 February snow storms descended over the front, and stopped the launch of the offensive dead in its tracks – the combination of heavy snow and fog meant that artillery fire-plans could not be implemented accurately, plus the conditions would hamper the advance of the attackers. Therefore the German troops, charged with adrenaline, were stood down. The delay stretched on for a total of ten days, the Germans having several frustrated alerts during this time. Their spirits were sapped by continuing life in the cold, dank *Stollen*, or in rough barracks further back, but they knew for certain that the day of the offensive would finally come. The French suffered under the same conditions, but did not realise that the weather was actually increasing their chances of surviving the battle. On 11 February, many of the units along the actual attack sector were still moving into position. Had three German corps descended upon them at that moment, rapid collapse would have been the likeliest outcome. As it was, the French front was still a thin crust compared to the German forces, but at least a useful level of manpower was in place.

On the evening of 20/21 February 1916, German meteorologists predicted a clear day to follow. Once again, the German troops were roused to action, and given their orders that the attack was about to commence. This time there would be no deferment, and one of the most concentrated episodes of slaughter in military history was about to begin.

THE BATTLEFIELD:
WHAT ACTUALLY HAPPENED?

At 4.00 a.m. on 21 February 1916, the Battle of Verdun opened with the deep thump of three 380mm naval guns opening fire, lobbing their sky-splitting shells deep behind the French frontlines. Their targets were bridges over the Meuse, the Bishop's Palace at Verdun, plus the city's railway station. The eruptions of the massive shells at point of impact were devastating, but as the frontlines were untouched, the men slowly roused themselves from slumber with the expectation of another quiet day in the trenches.

Then, as night gave way to dawn at around 7.00 a.m., hundreds of German artillery pieces and mortars unleashed a bombardment of soul-destroying ferocity. Such was the continual thunder of this barrage that it could be heard 241km (150 miles) away. For those on the receiving end, even for combat veterans, the experience was one of overwhelming, helpless horror. In minutes entire landscapes were re-contoured, turned inside out and moulded by tons of metal and explosive ripping into the earth. Driant's sector, for example, measured 1,300 x 800m (1,422 x 875yd) in area (Martin, *Verdun 1916*, p.33) but it received no fewer than 80,000 rounds. The experience of being under such a terrifying physical force was later recounted by a French infantryman:

*20. Refugees from bombarded Verdun. (*The Illustrated War News*,
15 March 1916)*

When you hear the whistling in the distance your entire body
preventively crunches together to prepare for the enormous
explosions. Every new explosion is a new attack, a new fatigue,
a new affliction. Even nerves of the hardest of steel are not
capable of dealing with this kind of pressure. The moment
comes when the blood rushes to your head, the fever burns
inside your body and the nerves, numbed with tiredness, are
not capable of reacting to anything anymore. It is as if you are
tied to a pole and threatened by a man with a hammer. First
the hammer is swung backwards in order to hit hard, then it
is swung forwards, only missing your skull by an inch, into the
splintering pole. In the end you just surrender. Even the strength
to guard yourself from splinters now fails you. There is even
hardly enough strength left to pray to God...

quoted in Wukovits, *World War I: Strategic Battles*, p.40

For the French, these first few hours of the battle were about
nothing more than survival. They hunkered into every trench,

dug-out, shellhole or other depression they could find, and trusted in nothing more than blind luck and meagre cover to keep them this side of death. The battering ranged far and wide along the French lines, running through the morning and into the afternoon. The nature of the bombardment gradually shifted its weight from the heavy-calibre howitzers to smaller field artillery and mortars, which delivered more precision targeting against positions that were still believed to hold opposition to the forthcoming German advance.

At 4.45 p.m., after a total of nine hours of unbelievable bombardment, German troops left their trenches and began the infantry assault across wrecked ground. Assault troops raced forward under the supporting fire of machine-guns, moving quickly in small groups, closing on the French trenches and showering them with grenades, or sending a jet of flamethrower-

*21. Verdun and environs: To the right, the cathedral towers mark the city; to the left, a shell is seen bursting. (*The Illustrated War News, *29 March 1916)*

powered burning oil along their length. Some positions fell without a fight, the defenders being too few to put up any sort of meaningful resistance. Yet this was not the case everywhere, and here were the seeds that made the Battle of Verdun an equal bloodbath for the Germans.

Driant's Defence and Douaumont's Fall

	21 February	4.00 a.m. – German artillery units begin their preparatory bombardment at Verdun
		4.45 a.m. – Bombardment ceases and the German infantry assault begins. The Bois d'Haumont and the Bois d'Herebois fall to the Germans, but Driant's Chasseurs just manage to hold on to the Bois des Caures
1916	22 February	The Germans renew their artillery bombardment at first light, then use a greater weight of forces to overwhelm the defence of the Bois des Caures. The hill is taken and Driant is killed
	23 February	Brabant is captured, and Samogneux's defence looks precarious. A French counter-attack to take the Bois des Caures fails
	24 February	The German advance takes several other key points, pushing the 51st Division off the Bois des Fosses and capturing Ornes village on the Meuse. The French second line of defences collapses
	25 February	Fort Douaumont is taken by the German 24th Infantry Regiment

During the terrifying nine-hour bombardment, the 1,300 men of the 56th and 59th Divisions suffered in the region of 60 per cent casualties. Men were interred in their trenches, buried alive by displaced earth, or physically rent asunder, their unrecognisable body parts scattered yards from the shell's impact point. Others died from shrapnel, or from the effects of blast alone, their lungs

*22. The destruction of a French church by German shells: The bombardment of Vaux-Devant-Damloup, near Verdun. (*The Illustrated War News*, 3 May 1916)*

destroyed without an outward mark on their bodies. Once the shelling stopped, however, dizzied survivors emerged and began an attempt to hold the line.

They faced the German 42nd Brigade, 21st Division, and did so with astonishing bravery given the experience of the last hours and the odds that they now faced – twelve battalions of enemy infantry. The machine-guns, rifles and grenades that weren't buried and still working were quickly put into action, and German troops began to fall. Individuals performed heroically to protect small outposts, fighting in small groups until killed, seriously wounded or out of ammunition. Ironically, the devastated landscape assisted the defence, creating a complicated terrain for the German attackers to move across. In some cases, French troops even mounted minor counter-attacks on outposts captured by the Germans.

In this way, Driant's men held onto much of the Bois des Caures until night fell, a shock to German troops who couldn't conceive that anyone, or anything, could have survived the bombardment they had unleashed. We should qualify this picture of French resistance a little by noting that only parts of the three German corps had been committed to these first stages of the battle; many troops were held back in expectation of an easy advance. Furthermore, progress had been made elsewhere. Either side the Bois des Caures, the Bois d'Haumont and the Bois d'Herebois were taken (although Haumont itself remained in French hands). The German forces were confident that their overwhelming superiority in numbers and firepower would take the field the next day.

Thus, on 22 February, the German guns once again opened fire en masse at first light, before the German troops were committed in far greater numbers. Haumont was taken in the late afternoon after a vicious street battle; only sixty-seven French soldiers of the battalion manning the village lived to surrender to the German VII Reserve Corps. The Germans had been nevertheless shocked by the trenchant, even reckless, nature of the resistance and they had suffered significant casualties. On the Bois des Caures, Driant and

*23. Wrecked buildings in the village of Douaumont. (*The Illustrated War News, *15 March 1916)*

24. *The French forces at Verdun were continually engaged in preparing, emplacing or repairing barbed-wire defences in the landscape.* (The Illustrated War News, *22 March 1916*)

his men continued to fight on, but the outcome was inevitable. The German troops swarmed over individual positions one by one, and during the French fighting retreat Driant himself was shot and killed. By the end of the day the Bois des Caures was in German hands, but the progress had been slow. At Beaumont, a village just south of the Bois des Caures, for example, the 208th Regiment held out against repeated German attacks and bombardments, although they then had to sit through the horror of shelling throughout the night-time hours.

The German progress at Verdun during the last week of February 1916 was slow enough to be frustrating for Falkenhayn, but steady enough to cause the French desperation. The penetrations after two days of fighting ranged from just 500m (547yd) at Ornes to 3,500m (3,828yd) at the Bois d'Haumont (Martin, *Verdun 1916*, p.40), and further victories came quickly. Brabant, on the Meuse, fell on 23 February, and a French attempt to recover the Bois des Caures failed with heavy casualties. Samogneux was taken the next day. On the 24th, the Bois des Fosses, Bois des Caures and Hill 344, all key positions, were added to the list of German acquisitions.

Another part of the plan that seemed to be bearing fruit was that the French were suffering from epic casualties. By the end of 24 February the French XXX Corps had lost more than 26,000 men. The 72nd Infantry Division alone had taken 9,828 casualties. Reinforcements were similarly roughly handled; the North African 37th Infantry Division lost 4,700 men dead, wounded or missing within just thirty-six hours of being deployed to the front on 24 February (Buckingham, *Verdun 1916: Battlefield Guide*, p.42). The net result was a precipitate collapse in morale. Indeed, Herr was seriously considering abandoning the right bank of the Meuse until orders from Joffre arrived, stating clearly that retreat was a policy that would lead to court-martial of those responsible. Nevertheless, confusion reigned, giving the Germans some instances of easy victories.

Fort Douaumont was a case in point. As the first of the Verdun fortifications in the line of the German advance, and the largest, Fort Douaumont would be a real prize for Falkenhayn and the Crown Prince. On the 24th, the German advance quickened in pace, pushing through the French second-line defences and driving towards Fort Douaumont, manned by just a few dozen men and armed with only two major guns. Given the scale of the German units surging around the fortification on the 25th, the outcome was a certainty. Fort Douaumont fell without armed resistance, and church bells later pealed in celebration across Germany as the news reached home. By this time, the German forces were just 1km (0.6 miles) from Fort Vaux. The French at Verdun appeared to require a miracle.

Pétain and the Beginnings of the French Recovery

We should remind ourselves that land grab was not necessarily the primary aim of Falkenhayn's strategy. Attrition was also a key objective, and on such a massive scale that it would effectively force the French out of the war. For this strategy to work, he needed the French to make a bold stand on the Meuse, feeding more and more men into the furnace. Falkenhayn would not be disappointed. The French would indeed fight to the death for Verdun, yet as events would show, attrition can work in both directions.

From a tactical point of view, abandoning Verdun to the Germans made much sense. By doing so the French could stem the immediate massive losses its battalions were suffering, plus it could take up new and more defensible positions near the Argonne. Furthermore, the retreat would put pressure on German supply lines. Already the German artillery in particular

25. *Mealtime in a French trench dug-out.* (The Illustrated War News, *19 April 1916)*

FIRST-HAND ACCOUNT – THE EFFECTS OF SHELL-SHOCK

We saw a handful of soldiers, commanded by a Captain, slowly approaching, one at the time. The Captain asked which company we were and then started to cry all of a sudden. Did he suffer of shellshock? Then he said: ... when I saw you approach it reminded me of six days ago, when I walked this same road with approximately a hundred men. And now look how few there are left ... We watched as we passed them; they were about twenty. They walked by us as living, plastered statues. Their faces stared at us like shrunken mummies, and their eyes were so immense that you could not see anything but their eyes...

German soldier, Wilhelm Hermanns

was beginning to experience problems in moving its guns forward with the advance. The German heavy guns were monsters – the 210mm howitzer, for example, weighed 4.7 tons – requiring both solid road surfaces and lots of space to move efficiently. By late February 1916, however, the roads were mushy, mud-soaked quagmires, and the French road system was limited. A French retreat, therefore, could be justified on several grounds.

It was not to be. A line was drawn in the sand by Pétain when he took over from a mentally collapsing Herr on 25 February, and the French prepared for a long struggle. Pétain, however, would not succumb to a crude calculus of attrition followed by many commanders. In fact, he put in place a judicious plan in which several key elements locked together in a tactical whole.

First, Pétain re-established Verdun's forts as the principal lines of defence (only Douaumont, after all, was in German hands), increasing their garrisons and firepower. The frontline of this defence was called the *position de barrage*; a fallback line on the forts Belleville, Souville, Tavannes and Moulainville was established further back, but only to be used in extremis. Once a solid defensive line was set, Pétain could plan to return to the offensive with the tens of thousands of fresh troops who were now to be poured into Verdun. Yet instead of favouring huge attacks with ambitious goals, Pétain framed his ambitions more around powerful but limited attacks, chipping away at the German strength until the time was propitious for a general push. Pétain also placed artillery at the centre of his battle plan, both in terms of the numbers of guns and in the numbers of shells delivered onto enemy lines on a daily basis. All artillery would be coordinated through meaningful fire plans, rather than acting in unilateral groups, and thus the concentrations of fire that could be delivered would be improved. Long-range attrition would be returned upon the Germans, plus their ability to manoeuvre, attack and resupply would be curtailed. (In terms of logistics, for example, French artillery killed 7,000 German supply horses in one day in February.) It should be noted that, by the end of February, the German Fifth Army had taken 25,000 casualties; it was not only the French who were eating into their manpower.

26. At Verdun: One of the reasons for General Pétain's confidence – batteries being held back in reserve. (The Illustrated War News, 22 March 1916)

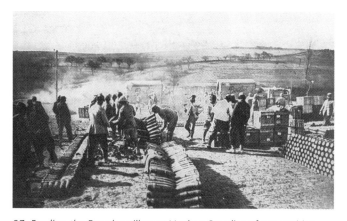

*27. Feeding the French artillery at Verdun: Supplies of ammunition conveyed to the batteries by motor lorry. (*The Illustrated War News, *5 April 1916)*

Pétain had the sagacity to realise that his whole strategy depended on good logistics. Here was the real threat, given that a single railway line (the more northerly line was now cut by German artillery) and narrow road were the only arterial routes to and from Verdun. Pétain turned responsibility for the road traffic over to one Major (Maj.) Richard, who set about conducting a logistical masterpiece. Cars, lorries and vans were requisitioned from all across France, and formed an immense, improvised fleet of supply vehicles. Horses were prohibited from using the road, to prevent the surface being damaged by hooves. The road itself was divided into six sections, each section overseen by units of mechanics, labourers, traffic control officers and supply masters, dedicated to keep the traffic on their section flowing smoothly. Any vehicles that broke down were immediately pushed off the road to maintain the flow, and troops heading for the front were also obliged to march in the fields adjacent to the roads, never on the road itself.

By rationalising the supply system in this way, Maj. Richard turned the road that led to Verdun into the famous *Voie Sacrée* (Sacred

28. *French efficiency in motor transport: A convoy of motor wagons on their way to the front with munitions.* (The Illustrated War News, *22 March 1916)*

29. *To pave the way for the guns: French motor vehicle transport logs for constructing roads for artillery, near Verdun.* (The Illustrated War News, *22 March 1916)*

Way), although this term was a post-war label to what was in 1916 more prosaically known as *la route*. Between 28 February and 7 March, the road was able to handle 25,000 tons of supplies, exceeding the minimum 2,000 tons a day required to maintain Verdun's survival. During the same period, 190,000 men moved up to the front.

Pétain's arrival was undoubtedly the salvation of Verdun. But this was just the beginning of the battle, and for tens of thousands of men, the journey up the *Voie Sacrée* would be the one of the last journeys they ever made.

Expanding the Battle

1916		
	4 March	Douaumont village falls to Germans
	6–9 March	German attack on west bank of the Meuse makes slow but steady progress, capturing Forges, Regnéville, the Bois des Courbeaux (recaptured on the 8th then lost again on the 10th) and Côte de l'Oie. Le Mort-Homme remains in French hands
	9 April	German forces launch a major attack on both sides of the Meuse. The onslaught on the west bank puts German troops on the slopes of Le Mort-Homme, but the offensive on the east bank makes little headway
	30 April	Pétain becomes commander of Army Group Centre; Nivelle takes over Second Army

By the beginning of March 1916, the German commanders at Verdun were aware that resistance was stiffening against them. Discussions between Falkenhayn, Crown Prince Wilhelm and Gen. Schmidt von Knobelsdorf (Wilhelm's chief of staff) resulted in a new plan, one that involved broadening the front of attack. A new offensive was conceived, delivered on both banks of the Meuse. On the west bank, the German VI Reserve Corps would make a major push to take Le Mort-Homme (The Dead Man), a vital ridge between Hill 304 and Cumières. Once this was taken, German artillery could be emplaced on the ridge to deliver more commanding fire against French artillery batteries firing on the east bank. As part of the attack, the VII Reserve Corps would attempt a river crossing from the east to west bank in the north of the sector. At the same time as the troops moved down the west bank, the forces on the east bank would renew their attempt to capture Fort Vaux.

Severe winter weather imposed another delay on proceedings, essentially reducing the battlefield to little more than an artillery duel for a week. The new offensive began on 6 March, once again with a preparatory bombardment of shattering intensity. The difference this time was that the French forces were ready, with four new divisions deployed forward and a proper artillery counter-battery plan in place. Thousands of shells scorched past each other in opposite directions in the wintry air over Verdun, shattering further what were once pretty villages or contemplative stretches of Lorraine countryside.

30. At Verdun: An unexploded German shell enclosed in wire netting to prevent accidental discharge by French soldiers. (The Illustrated War News, 22 March 1916)

The German infantry attack began at 10.00 a.m. Between this moment and the end of day on 7 March, the Germans on the west bank encircled Béthincourt, took Forges, Regnéville, the Bois de Corbeaux and its Point 265, a vital piece of high ground with an integral tactical relationship to Le Mort-Homme. Such was the importance of this feature that at first light on 8 March the French 92nd Regiment, led by the urbane Lt Col Macker, counter-attacked and retook the hill. Point 265 became the centre of a two-day struggle for occupation that the Germans eventually won, securing the Bois de Corbeaux but at the cost of heavy casualties. Macker himself died on 10 March, leading yet another attack. When the day ended, the 92nd Regiment had almost ceased to exist as a meaningful combat formation.

For the next ten days, intense fighting continued as the Germans tried to make advances, pushing onwards into the face of punishing artillery fire and accurate rifle and machine-gun fire. On the 20th, however, a well-planned attack by the 11th Bavarian Division broke the French resistance. The French 29th Infantry Division, holding a

31. A French field searchlight on its travelling carriage, waiting to be moved to the firing line. (The Illustrated War News, 19 April 1916)

crucial line in the Bois d'Avocourt and Bois d'Malancourt just a few miles west of Hill 304, were routed. The Germans had taken most of their objectives, but again at heavy cost.

On the east bank the German attack towards Fort Vaux also found the French soldiers in stubborn mood. It took the rest of the month to subdue Vaux village, the scene of no fewer than thirteen attacks and counter-attacks, and an attempt to take Fort Vaux itself was blasted into defeat by the defenders. The successful defence of Fort Vaux was a welcome boost to French morale, lauded in the newspapers and newsreels as a clear sign that the vitality was now starting to ebb out from the German offensive at Verdun.

For the soldiers on the frontlines, there would have been little sign of diminishing action, although from mid-March to 9 April the front became the scene of multiple smaller attacks and counter-attacks, as each side struggled to gain dominance over significant features in the landscape. The Germans acquired a few more localised victories – Malancourt village on 31 March, Haucourt on 5 April and Béthincourt on 8 April.

32. Air torpedoes at Verdun: A French soldier preparing to fire one under the direction of an officer. (The Illustrated War News, 19 April 1916)

DID YOU KNOW?

On 8 May an accidental explosion at Fort Douaumont triggered the detonation of the entire ammunition magazine, the subsequent blast killing 679 Germans. It was thought the catastrophe began when soldiers brewed a pot of coffee on a box containing hand grenades.

33. Effects of French heavy guns near Verdun: Remains of a captured German trench wrecked by bombardment. (The Illustrated War News, 22 March 1916)

The Germans were advancing, but at a rate that placed Verdun itself months, even years, out of reach. Moreover, the attrition equation favoured the Germans, but only just – the German forces on the west bank of the Meuse alone had taken 81,607 casualties, as against 89,000 French. One German attack on 22 March cost 2,400 men.

*34. Paris motor buses about to head out to the frontline to deliver provisions. (*The Illustrated War News*, 15 March 1916)*

Falkenhayn reordered his command structure at Verdun as he prepared for another big push. German forces west of the Meuse were now led by Gen. Max von Gallwitz and those east of the river by Gen. Bruno von Mudra, both veterans of many hard-fought campaigns. The new offensive of 9 April was a coordinated attempt to break French resistance across the front, and a five-division attack on the left bank of the Meuse succeeded in securing German troops on the north-eastern slope of Le Mort-Homme. Fighting around Douaumont was far less profitable, and the mismatch between the limited ground gained for the heavy casualties incurred led to Falkenhayn replacing von Mudra with Gen. Ewald von Lochow. The French launched their own counter-attacks on the east bank on 11 April and 17 April, but the frontline was little changed by the effort.

On 30 April, an important change occurred in the French command structure around Verdun. With massive forces deployed to Verdun – fifty-two divisions by the end of April – Joffre was becoming rattled at the apparent lack of progress. He felt frustration at what he perceived as Pétain's offensive caution, and particularly his practice of rotating French units out of the line every few days to preserve their mental and physical health under the strain of battle. Joffre felt that this didn't encourage sufficient aggression, but Pétain's popularity amongst his men meant that he couldn't simply be replaced. Instead Joffre promoted Pétain to the higher command of Army Group Centre, and brought in the fiery Nivelle as chief of Second Army. Now Joffre hoped to see some of the commitment he desired, and Pétain watched as his careful models of organisation and efficiency were unravelled.

The Grinding Mill

4–24 May	German forces make repeated attacks on Le Mort-Homme	
22 May	A French counter-attack against Fort Douaumont by the 5th Infantry Division fails	
29 May– 2 June	Fighting is intense around Hill 304, Le Mort-Homme and Thiaumont	
3–8 June	Fort Vaux is surrounded by the Germans, and after a five-day battle the French are forced to surrender this key position	
23–30 June	A major German attack in the Thiaumont–Fleury–Souville sector brings further German gains, although the impending Anglo-French offensive on the Somme begins to pull German attention further north	
1 July	Battle of the Somme begins	
11–12 July	The final major German offensive of Operation Gericht fails to take Souville	

1916

For much of May the focus remained on Le Mort-Homme, scene of almost constant fighting as the Germans attempted to push out from the north-eastern slopes. Yet the war was still highly active on the other bank and, on 22 May, Mangin launched his 5th Infantry Division against Fort Douaumont after a pounding five-day artillery barrage against the fortification. Despite his belligerent spirit, Mangin had planned the attack with some care and thought, and, incredibly, his troops managed to occupy the devastated roof area of the fort, as the German garrison hid in the fume-filled corridors and rooms below. The switch from victory to defeat came quickly, however. German intelligence intercepts had forewarned Falkenhayn of the attack, and during the initial attack Mangin's regiments had been massively depleted – entire battalions had been virtually wiped out – and a further attack by the 124th Infantry against the German frontline did nothing but add another 500 casualties to the lists. German artillery severed Mangin's troops from reinforcements, then a counter-attack swept the surviving French troops from Fort Douaumont. What was intended by Mangin as a bravura demonstration of the offensive spirit turned into the near destruction of the 5th Infantry Division. A total of 6,400 men were killed, wounded, missing or taken prisoner.

Over on the German side, Wilhelm was beginning to doubt the viability of the Verdun operation. Falkenhayn recognised the reticence, hence Wilhelm's chief of staff, Schmidt von Knobelsdorf, increasingly took the operational authority for Fifth Army. During the month of May the German forces on the west bank finally brought Hill 304 and Le Mort-Homme under control, and now the emphasis would shift back to the east bank. The army's next major offensive was known as Operation May Cup. In this action, five divisions of I Bavarian, X Reserve and XV Reserve Corps were

DID YOU KNOW?

During the five-day bombardment of Fort Douaumont before Mangin's offensive on 22 May, the French artillery were dropping a total of 1,000 tons of shells each day on the fortification.

*35. French soldiers repairing wire entanglements. (*The Illustrated War News, *24 May 1916)*

to capture key positions on the road to Verdun itself, principally Thiaumont, Fleury, Fort Vaux and Fort Souville. Once these were safely in German hands, then the Fifth Army could make the final punch through Verdun's innermost ring of fortifications, and the city was there for the taking.

Operation May Cup began on 1 June, in classic fashion. The French frontline positions disappeared under a storm of shell, and nowhere came in for more deadly consideration than Fort Vaux. Vaux was one of the more diminutive of the Verdun fortifications, about a quarter of the size of Douaumont. By the time of the German assault, it had already been cruelly shelled. Its only remaining 75mm gun had been destroyed (the four other 75mm guns had been removed in 1915, replaced by machine-guns) and its reinforced concrete roof was severely cracked by the detonations of 420mm rounds. At least the fort, and its three outlying strongpoints (*Retranchement* 1–3) were fully

*36. Drinking water for the frontline trenches. (*The Illustrated War News, *24 May 1916)*

garrisoned, commanded by Maj. Sylvain-Eugene Raynal of the 142nd Regiment. In fact, because of the influx of men (including wounded) from other positions on the east bank, Fort Vaux was actually packed with 600 personnel, as opposed to the 250 it was designed for.

At the height of the German bombardment on 1 June 1916, Fort Vaux was taking about 2,000 shells per hour. When it stopped, the German troops attacked on a 5km (3-mile) front through the Bois de la Caillette and Bois de Fumin, where the three strongpoints were located. Progress on the first day, however, was far greater than the Germans expected. The R2 and R3 strongpoints were rapidly subdued, and R1 was effectively cut off and unable to influence the battle to any significant degree (it would finally fall to the Germans on 9 June). By the end of the first day, therefore, the German troops were beginning their assault on Vaux itself, three days earlier than planned. The approach to the fort was costly for the Germans, courtesy of long-range machine-gun fire (the 53rd Regiment's machine-gun company was one of the units taking refuge at Fort Vaux). There was also appalling fighting in

37. Light railways were used by the French for transporting the wounded to a field ambulance. Here we see a stretcher case on a truck. (The Illustrated War News, 5 April 1916)

and around the fort's moat, which was protected by two flanking galleries called *coffres*, set up to deliver enfilading fire. Both were eventually destroyed with demolition charges and flamethrowers, and German assault troops penetrated the subterranean interior of the fort, where hand-to-hand battles took place in the smoky half-light.

The battle for Fort Vaux raged for a total of eight days. On numerous occasions the French troops fought off penetrations by German engineers and assault troops, or endured the suffocating blast of flamethrowers down the confined tunnels. On 6 June, four French companies of the 238th and 321st Regiments attempted a relief operation, Raynal having informed Gen. Lebrun that the fort's water supplies were nearly completely gone. The counter-attack failed, and at 6.00 a.m. on 8 June Raynal finally surrendered the fort, his men reduced to licking moisture from the walls in an attempt to slake their thirst. Another counter-attack the following day, conceived by Nivelle and using colonial regiments, was brutally repelled, the units suffering from heavy shelling even before they launched their attack.

The May Cup attack had seen much heavy fighting outside Fort Vaux. Thiaumont, the site of a major *ouvrage* (fortification) and an important position controlling the approaches to Souville, for example, was captured by the Germans on 1 June, recaptured by the French the next day, then changed ownership no fewer than fourteen times over the summer months, making it one of the bloodiest sectors of the Verdun front. By the end of June, following a major seventeen-regiment attack in the sector on 23 June, the Thiaumont redoubt was in German hands.

Yet now the entire strategic situation was about to change. On 1 July 1916, after a preparatory bombardment to rival anything delivered by Operation Gericht, the British and French launched their Somme offensive further north. This mighty battle, which rivalled Gericht in terms of scale and slaughter, was to have a profound influence on the development of events at

38. 'Hecatombs' – Sacrificed to the moloch of Prussian militarism: Massed infantry attacking at Verdun mown down by the French guns. (The Illustrated War News, 29 March 1916. Drawn by Frederic de Haenen)

*39. A French bivouac in a church in the environs of Verdun. (*The Illustrated War News, *19 April 1916)*

PHOSGENE GAS

The Germans utilised large volumes of phosgene gas during the Battle of Verdun. Phosgene gas acted as a deadly choking agent, and had twice the lethality of chlorine gas. It initially caused less coughing than chlorine gas when inhaled, meaning that larger volumes were breathed in before the victim began to experience the worst effects.

Verdun. With a major threat to the German line further north, Falkenhayn was obliged to draw away reserve forces and artillery units from Verdun, weakening the momentum of constant attack. Furthermore, attrition was biting hard on both sides at Verdun, and the Somme would add a further 500,000 German casualties as it ran its course through the summer, autumn and into the winter of 1916.

Unknown to the French, the final German offensive action of the Battle of Verdun was about to begin. Initiated by

Knobelsdorf upon a now-reticent Falkenhayn, the attack was to be thrust at Fort Souville, delivered in a two-pronged fashion from Fleury and the Fort Vaux area. A preparatory assault to capture the Damloup Battery – an obstacle in the way of the eastern advance against Fort Souville – was successful on 3 July, but poor weather postponed the main assault from 9 July to 11 July, plus turned the battlefield into a now-familiar quagmire that would retard movement on both sides. Ironically, when the attack was actually launched, after a deluge of high-explosive and gas shells upon the French lines, Falkenhayn had actually called off the action, but his orders did not reach the frontline divisional HQs in time enough to stop the German troops clambering from their trenches and beginning the deadly journey towards Fort Souville.

The action was a typically bloody affair for both sides. The first day brought German advances of up to 365m (400yds), although with extremely heavy losses to the 3rd Jäger Regiment and 140th Infantry Regiment attacking from Fleury, caught in French artillery fire. The next day, a small group of German infantrymen were separated from their main forces and actually surmounted the roof of Fort Souville, leading to some German observers thinking the fortress had been taken. They were soon pushed off by a French counter-attack, and by the end of the day the German advance had effectively run out of steam. Although the battle had months to run, Operation Gericht as an offensive action had now ceased, and the city of Verdun itself remained just out of reach, about 3km (2 miles) beyond the German frontline.

Recovery

1916		
	28 August	Falkenhayn resigns, and is replaced by Paul von Hindenburg
	2 September	Hindenburg orders that all offensive operations at Verdun cease
	19 October	French artillery begins a major preparatory bombardment of the German lines at Verdun
	24 October	Major French offensive begins, making advances of 3km (1.8 miles) on the first day, and recapturing Fort Douaumont
	2 November	French forces recapture Fort Vaux
	15 December	Another French offensive at Verdun pushes German forces back almost to their February 1916 start positions

It was now nearly five months since the German Army had launched its epic offensive on the Western Front. The casualties on both sides amounted to more than 500,000 men, and the landscape had undergone a torture that virtually defied description. A letter written by a German soldier of the 65th Infantry Division in July 1916 stated the human cost in unflinching terms:

> Anyone who has not seen these fields of carnage will never be able to imagine it. When one arrives here the shells are raining down everywhere with each step one takes but in spite of this it is necessary for everyone to go forward. One has to go out of one's way not to pass over a corpse lying at the bottom of the communication trench. Farther on, there are many wounded to tend, others who are carried back on stretchers to the rear. Some are screaming, others are pleading. One sees some who don't have legs, others without any heads, who have been left for several weeks on the ground...

The conditions for both French and German troops on the Verdun front were almost universally ghastly, and they would remain so for months yet. The fighting continued with intensity around Verdun throughout the summer and into the early autumn. Explaining each clash in detail is beyond the scope of this book – Fleury alone changed hands sixteen times between 23 June and 18 August (when it fell into French hands for the final time) – and other locations experienced similar wrestling matches. Furthermore, despite the fact that large volumes of German artillery had been siphoned off to the Somme sector, high-explosive shells arced through the Verdun sector skies every day, further obliterating the landscape and adding to the death toll with dismal regularity.

Yet the strategic situation was now changed utterly. To the French it had become clear that the steam had gone out of the German offensive. On 3 August, Joffre issued a public statement that bristled with defiance and a sense of opportunity:

40. Relief column on its way to the frontlines at Verdun. (The War Budget, *16 March 1916)*

Thiaumont, 5 August 1916

Official French record of one day's fighting

On the east bank of the Meuse fighting continued all day in the Thiaumont-Fleury region. To the northwest and to the south of the Thiaumont work all enemy attacks undertaken to dislodge us from the positions captured were vain. Not only did we break the enemy's efforts and inflict on him heavy losses, but by means of a second return offensive our troops succeeded in capturing for the second time in twelve hours the Thiaumont work, which remains in our power in spite of several counter-attacks made by the enemy. (Fifth French recapture.)

Quoted in Horne, *Source Records*, 1923

The great sacrifices which France has supported at Verdun have given our Allies time to build up their resources, have enabled us to mature our plans and carry them out with perfect appreciation of the necessities of all fronts...

The five months' resistance of the French troops at Verdun has shattered the plans of the German Staff, and brought us round the corner, heading for victory. Don't, however, imagine that there is yet a marked weakening of the German effort on the western front. Two-thirds of their finest troops are still opposed to us on this side. The English and French face 122 of their best divisions. On the Russian front the Germans have 50 divisions to which must, of course, be added the Austrian armies.

I won't go into details on the condition and temper of the French army. You cannot do better than avail yourself of the facilities to see our troops in the field with your own eyes. You will see the army as it is after two years of the hardest fighting.

You will see an army of which the spirit and energy have been
vastly increased by this bitter struggle.

Quoted in Horne, *Source Records*, 1923

Joffre's sense that the French Army had turned 'round the corner'
was reflected in plans for a major counter-offensive. Even as
the daily battles rumbled on along the Verdun frontline, Pétain
began bringing together the ingredients to reverse the battle.
This involved reigning in hotheads such as Mangin, who wasted
much of the 37th Infantry Division in costly attacks on Fleury.
At the same time, Pétain built up an offensive resource of eight
divisions of troops and 650 artillery pieces. Regarding artillery, by
the end of August 1916 the French had achieved parity with the
Germans, and for the forthcoming offensive they also had the
earth-shaking resources of two 400mm Schneider-Creusot railway
guns. Planned for October 1916, the offensive aimed to take back
territory north of the Côte de Froidterre, recapturing the critical
Thiaumont Farm position, the Ravin de la Couleuvre, Fort Vaux

*41. French artillery depot behind the Verdun battle zone. (*The Illustrated
War News, *15 March 1916)*

Flight over Verdun

Immediately east and north of Verdun there lies a broad, brown band... Peaceful fields and farms and villages adorned that landscape a few months ago – when there was no Battle of Verdun. Now there is only that sinister brown belt, a strip of murdered Nature. It seems to belong to another world. Every sign of humanity has been swept away. The woods and roads have vanished like chalk wiped from a blackboard; of the villages nothing remains but grey smear where stone walls have tumbled together. The great forts of Douaumont and Vaux are outlined faintly, like that tracings of a finger in wet sand. One cannot distinguish any one shell crater, as one can on the pockmarked fields on either side. On the brown band the indentations are so closely interlocked that they blend into a confused mass of troubled earth. Of the trenches only broken, half-obliterated links are visible.

Columns of muddy smoke spurt up continually as high explosives tear deeper into this ulcered [*sic*] area. During heavy bombardment and attacks I have seen shells falling like rain... A smoky pall covers the sector under fire, rising so high that at a height of 1,000 feet one is enveloped in its mist-like fumes. Now and then monster projectiles hurtling through the air close by leave one's plane rocking violently in their wake. Airplanes have been cut in two by them.

For us the battle passes in silence, the noise of one's motor deadening all other sounds. In the green patches behind the brown belt myriads of tiny flashes tell where the guns are hidden; and those flashes, and a smoke of bursting shells, are all we see of the fighting. It is a weird combination of stillness and havoc, the Verdun conflict viewed from the sky.

James McConnell, *Flying for France*, New York, 1916

*42. One of France's famous motor guns in action dropping shells into the German lines 5km (3 miles) away. (*The War Budget, *16 March 1916)*

and Fort Douaumont, widening the protective buffer between the German frontline and Verdun.

As these preparations were underway, there were command changes amongst the German forces. By August 1916 it was evident that Gericht had failed to achieve its strategic objectives. French resilience appeared undiminished, while the German capacity to prosecute the campaign was enervated by its losses and the drain placed on manpower by the Battle of the Somme to the north. Vigorous arguments brewed up amongst the German high command about the right policy. The Crown Prince, backed by local commanders such as Gen. von Lochow, supported adopting a defensive strategy to reduce German losses while continuing to inflict attrition upon the French. Falkenhayn was not in favour of a return to the major offensives of February–July, but he did give Knobelsdorf and Gen. von Francois the permission to maintain aggressive operations. Matters came to a head in late August, when the Crown Prince fired Knobelsdorf. Lochow took over responsibility for the Fifth Army, while in September Wilhelm would go on to take command of Army Group Crown Prince in the central part of the German frontline. Falkenhayn's enemies were

MEMORANDUM BY GENERAL VON ZWEHL, OCTOBER 1916

The value of Fort Douaumont, leaving aside the great political importance of its possession by us, lies in the possibility of our artillery dominating the terrain in front of it, thanks to the excellent observation posts in its armoured turrets.

We can only prevent a surprise of our first line by its means. Moreover, to a certain extent, the fort gives our reserves good shelter two kilometres from our first line. According to information from agents a French attack on the Verdun front is to be expected. Our battle position must be held at all costs. Infantry and machine guns must be ready to repulse French attacks at any moment. The greatest number of grenades must be carried to the front line, the reserves and machine gun reserves at Thiaumont–Hang and Ablain–Schlucht and Minzenschlucht must be prepared to go to the front line at any moment.

Quoted in Horne, *Source Records*, 1923

also now circling, scenting blood. On 28 August, the day after Romania entered the war on the side of the Allies, Falkenhayn resigned, having failed to predict correctly the timetable of the Romanian decision and having lost the confidence of the Kaiser in his prosecution of the Verdun campaign. FM Hindenburg stepped into his shoes, and on 2 September he ordered that all offensive operations at Verdun cease. If ever there was a signal admission of the failure of Operation Gericht, here it was.

The October Offensive

The French offensive at Verdun in October 1916 was a dramatic reversal of the situation that had eclipsed the Verdun sector the previous February. Now it was the turn of the Germans to hunker down in fortified shelters; those in forts such as Douaumont had to rely on the same protection as their previous French occupiers, although this time the structures had been profoundly weakened by months of bombardment. The offensive was originally scheduled for 17 October but, in what was now something of a tradition, bad weather postponed the start date to 22 October.

French artillery had been softening up the German positions since 3 October, but on 19 October the preparatory barrage began in earnest. The pounding, delivered expertly by the French batteries, was devastating. A deliberate momentary pause in the bombardment brought German return fire for just long enough to target the positions of the German batteries via aerial reconnaissance; seventy-two of the batteries were subsequently destroyed by precise counter-battery fire. Fort Douaumont was mercilessly struck by the prodigious shells from the French railway guns, which punched through the weakened superstructure like Thor's hammer and caused devastation inside. One shell, which hit on 23 October at 12.30 p.m., penetrated through to the sick bay before exploding, killing sixty of the occupants. Those who had survived to this point staggered around in a choking, infernal environment.

The actual infantry assault began at dawn on 24 September, the first wave of troops consisting of the 38th, 74th and 177th Infantry Divisions, plus a regiment of colonial infantry. (Three more divisions would act as the second wave, and two divisions sat in reserve.) French troops moved so fast across no man's land that

Did you know?

The shells fired from the French 400mm railway guns each weighed more than a metric tonne.
They fired at Fort Douamont from a range of about 10km (6 miles).

*43. German prisoners at Verdun: One of the batches lined up in a village for General Joffre's inspection. (*The Illustrated War News, *22 March 1916)*

many of them cast off their packs to enable them to run faster. The day was to be an astonishing one of advance. Fleury, Thiaumont, Haudromont quarries and Fort Douaumont all fell within the day. Resistance from the weary, demoralised German troops was patchy. Some sectors, such as the Haudromont quarries, fought hard against the French gains, inflicting heavy casualties on the French attackers in the process. Fort Douaumont, by contrast, was taken by the *Régiment d'Infanterie Coloniale du Maroc* by surprise with scarcely a shot fired and only fourteen casualties, such was the disorder and disorientation of the defenders. A French account of the battle captures the vivid sights of the day:

> From the slopes of Souville I have seen victory climb and crown Douaumont.

Our modern battles afford no spectacle; they are cruel and mysterious. There are big empty spaces clotted with shell holes and cut with long furrows which mark the soil as the veins make marble patterns on the hands. There are columns of smoke from bursting shells, a line of shadows that creeps close to the earth and disappears. Those who are in the battle never know anything more of it than one episode. But the victory of October 24th – I saw it before me like a living being.

Every now and again I pulled out my watch. Eleven o'clock! Eleven-twenty! Eleven-forty! The time fixed! Had the attack, which I ought to have seen rise up and roll down the ravine and then sweep over the opposing slope, had it been launched? Had the artillery lengthened its fire?

It was impossible to know. At eleven-fifty on the right I heard the tick-tick of machine guns. If machine guns were in action the attack must have been launched. If machine guns are firing our men have been seen and are meeting with resistance.

Then I heard them no more. The roar of the guns drowned everything and again I go through uncertainty and anxiety. At the command post where I went from time to time news was at last coming through.

The start was magnificent. The first objective is reported to have been reached already. The men are organising their positions. They are going to get on the move again. They are off.

Quoted in Horne, *Source Records*, 1923

On 24 September alone, the French forces at Verdun advanced 3km (1.8 miles) and took more than 6,000 prisoners. Mangin – the commander of the offensive – now found an ideal outlet for his offensive spirit, and the French pressure continued on the German lines. Fort Vaux fell on 2 November, the German garrison having abandoned it hours before. Almost all of the territory captured by the Germans since the beginning of Gericht was now in French hands, but Pétain looked to secure the job with

*44. German prisoners working under a French guard. (*The Illustrated War News*, 7 June 1916)*

another major attack. This eight-division offensive was launched on 15 December after another bruising artillery bombardment, courtesy of 760 artillery pieces. The German defenders were in an even weaker position than they were three weeks previously, and for relatively inconsequential losses the French took the Côte du Poivre, Hill 342 and Vacherauville, and another 11,000 Germans went into captivity. By mid-December, therefore, the German frontline was now 8km (5 miles) from the city of Verdun. The city was essentially beyond danger once again, and the French could declare themselves victors in the battle.

AFTER THE BATTLE

At the approach of Christmas 1916, it was time for all sides to take stock of what had occurred at Verdun. For the Germans, the lessons were naturally negative. The battle had indeed become an exercise in attrition, but in the final accounting the balance was scarcely in the Germans' favour. Total German casualties sustained at Verdun in 1916 were 329,000 men, of which 142,000 were fatalities or missing. French casualties amounted to 156,000 dead or missing and 195,000 wounded, a total of 351,000 casualties. At this scale, the fact that the Germans had lost some 20,000 fewer men mattered little – Falkenhayn had bled his own army as much as the enemy's forces.

The German post-mortem on what went wrong at Verdun began well before the French offensive of October 1916, or the final victories of December. A later account of the battle written by Ludendorff, even taking into account his natural antipathy towards Falkenhayn, nevertheless makes some sound judgements:

> The position of our attacking troops grew more and more unfavourable. The more ground they gained, the deeper they plunged into the wilderness of shell-holes, and apart from

actual losses in action, they suffered heavy wastage merely through having to stay in such a spot, not to mention the difficulty of getting up supplies over a wide, desolate area. The French enjoyed a great advantage here, as the proximity of the fortress [Verdun] gave them a certain amount of support. Our attacks dragged on, sapping our strength. The very men who had first fought so heroically at Verdun were now terrified of this shell-ravaged region. The command had not their hearts in their work. The Crown Prince had very early declared himself in favour of breaking off the attack. That offensive should have been broken off immediately it assumed the character of a battle of attrition. The gain no longer justified the losses.

Quoted in Horne, *Source Records*, 1923

Ludendorff identifies some factors about the Battle of Verdun that were shared by many sectors of the Western Front. One of the most important was the issue of supply and movement in a landscape utterly wrecked by incessant shellfire. Frontline troops not only became starved of supplies in many positions (during the October offensive, some German prisoners claimed that they had not received food for six days), but they also became weakened in health and morale by the dreadful living conditions. Whereas French troops were generally rotated out of the line every two weeks, the Germans would remain in position for months, the daily experience chipping away at their ability to resist. Furthermore, once the offensive movement drained out of Operation Gericht, the French artillery could deliver a constant rain of death on German heads.

Ludendorff might also have mentioned broader German tactical mistakes during the offensive phase. Reserves were kept back when committing them might have turned the course of a battle, and the offensive was often launched over too narrow a front, preventing a general collapse of the French lines. Ludendorff also points out the obvious problem that the German commanders at Verdun 'had not their hearts in the work', identifying the Crown

Prince in particular. It was certainly the case that enthusiasm for the Verdun offensive had waned amongst many in the high command by July 1916. Looking at the offensive in its broadest strokes, the objectives for the operation appear to be drawn very loosely, with uncertain objectives. Questions still remain over what Gericht was actually for – the capture of Verdun (territorial objective) or to inflict attrition (human objective). It is likely to have been somewhere between the two, but historically a lack of clear mission objective has been the downfall of many an army.

45. 'The Road-bed' – cartoon depicting the slaughter at Verdun. (The War Budget, 30 March 1916. New York Evening Telegram)

Little wonder, therefore, that commanders such as the Crown Prince quickly lost heart in the campaign once the attrition on the German side began to mount.

The post-war period offered the opportunity for many commanders to write history in their favour. Exculpatory purposes mean that we have to take many of the documents with a pinch of salt, but another useful account is that written by Hindenburg in 1920, in his book *Out of my Life*. In this work, he outlines the reasons for which he called off the Verdun offensive:

> Very soon after I took over my new post I found myself compelled by the general situation to ask His Majesty the Emperor to order the offensive at Verdun to be broken off. The battles there exhausted our forces like an open wound. Moreover, it was obvious that in any case the enterprise had become hopeless, and that for us to persevere with it would cost us greater losses than those we were able to inflict on the enemy.
>
> Our forward zone was at all points exposed to the flanking fire of superior hostile artillery. Our communications with the battle-line were extremely difficult. The battlefield was a regular hell and regarded as such by the troops.
>
> When I look back now, I do not hesitate to say that on purely military grounds it would have been far better for us to have improved our situation at Verdun by the voluntary evacuation of the ground we had captured.
>
> In August, 1916, however, I considered I could not adopt that course. To a large extent the flower of our best fighting troops had been sacrificed in the enterprise. The public at home still anticipated a glorious issue to the offensive.
>
> It would be only too easy to produce the impression that all these sacrifices had been incurred in vain. Such an impression I was anxious to avoid in the existing state of public opinion, nervous enough as it already was.
>
> Quoted in Horne, *Source Records*, 1923

Here Hindenburg acknowledges the weariness of the German troops, plus the detrimental effects of the increasingly confident French artillery. The uneven nature of the advance also meant the German troops in the Douaumont–Fleury–Damloup triangle were faced with French artillery on all sides, meaning that any resumption of the attack would face enfilading fire from their western flank. What is most striking about the passage above, at least to modern eyes, is that Hindenburg rejects a straightforward retreat for reasons of morale – the 'sacrifices' of the men had to be shown to count for something, even if the continued prosecution of the battle would cost thousands more lives. Hindenburg goes on to admit that, eventually, the German resolve was broken by an increasingly competent French handling of offensive tactics:

We were disappointed in our hopes that with the breaking-off of our offensive at Verdun the enemy would more or less confine himself to purely trench warfare there. At the end of October the French opened a largely-conceived and boldly-executed counter-attack on the eastern bank of the Meuse, and overran our lines. We lost Douaumont, and had no longer the strength to recover that field of honour of German heroism.

For this attack the French commander had abandoned the former practice of an artillery preparation extending over days or even weeks. By increasing the rate of fire of the artillery and trench-mortars to the extreme limit of capacity of material and men, only a short period of preparation had preceded the attack, which had then been launched immediately against the physically exhausted and morally shaken defenders.

We had already had experience of this enemy method of preparation for the attack in the course of the long attrition battles, but as the herald to a great infantry attack it was a novelty to us, and it was perhaps just this feature which doubtless produced so important a success.

Taking it all round, on this occasion the enemy hoisted us with our own petard. We could only hope that in the coming year he would not repeat the experiment on a greater scale and with equal success.

Quoted in Horne, *Source Records*, 1923

Here we might find something of a justification for the French philosophy of *offensive á outrance* (to the uttermost), the French eventually prevailing through a dynamism that the weakened Germans could not match. Yet, if anything, Hindenburg is acknowledging the technical as much as tactical innovations of the French high command. Artillery became the brutal pulse of the battle, and once the French had achieved parity to the German guns, and developed efficient coordination between powerful bombardments and rapid infantry assaults, it was hard for the German defenders to resist the momentum building up against them in the late summer and early autumn of 1916.

46. Heavy artillery, such as these siege guns held in reserve, were critical to the French victory at Verdun. (The Illustrated War News, 19 April 1916)

Tired Victors

We might think that the French victory at Verdun brought celebration, and it is true that the French propaganda machine worked hard to convince the French people of the campaign's success. Across the ranks of the French Army, however, bitterness took hold. Verdun had robbed nearly 330,000 French men of either their lives or their health, cutting a swathe of grief and suffering through a population that had already lost more than a million of its young men. For many observers, Joffre's lack of response to the growing evidence of an impending German offensive at Verdun in late 1915 and early 1916 bordered on the criminal, and wore away some of the store of good will he had built up following the Marne victory. On 13 December 1916, he was replaced with Gen. Robert Nivelle.

Events of the following year illustrate what a poor choice Nivelle was for an emotionally and physically drained French Army. On 16 April 1917, Nivelle launched a massive offensive along the Chemin des Dames ridge; lax security from the French meant that the Germans had received plenty of advance warning about the offensive, and had prepared their defences accordingly. The subsequent losses amongst the French infantry were appalling – nearly 140,000 casualties in little over a week. Small flames of mutiny were lit amongst the French soldiery, but these spread until, by May/June 1917, up to 40,000 French soldiers were in rebellion. Pétain – a trusted figure amongst the *poilu* – had to step into the situation and quell the rebellion with a mixture of carrot and stick. The stick included twenty-seven men executed and hundreds more sentenced to long prison terms, but the carrot was Pétain's genuine ear to grievances. He visited ninety divisions personally to talk to the men, established regular periods of rest for frontline soldiers (rather than spending their rest periods working as behind-the-lines labourers), improved supplies and put in place better care provisions for bereaved families. It also became obvious that Nivelle was not fit for commanding this fragile army, for tactical as well as humanitarian reasons. Pétain became chief of staff on 29 April, and on 15 May dismissed Nivelle from his post, sending him conveniently out the way to serve in Africa.

The mutinies of 1917 indicate the state of mind of the French Army following months of extreme sacrifice at Verdun, through which sector a total of 75 per cent of the entire army had passed between February and December 1916. Nor should the outcome mask the reality of what a close-run battle it had been. Had not the Somme offensive drawn German manpower and artillery off to the north, the victory might indeed have eventually fallen to the Germans, although, given the static nature of much of the Western Front, that is far from certain. The French had in many

*47. Supplies of French heavy shells on their way to the firing line: Motor ammunition wagons on the road. (*The Illustrated War News, *22 March 1916)*

ways responded in full accordance with a German strategy of attrition (if indeed that was the overarching aim), pushing hundreds of thousands of troops up the *Voie Sacrée* and using their bodies to protect objectives of questionable value. However, as Hindenburg noted about the German side above, once the French were committed to Verdun's defence, then retreating from it was inconceivable.

The conditions experienced by the French soldiers on the frontlines were nearly beyond imagination. Indeed, if there was one, albeit hollow, victory the Germans could claim from Verdun was that it dealt a near catastrophic blow to the overall morale of the French Army, a blow repeated with the brutally prosecuted Nivelle Offensive in 1917. While this book has necessarily taken a higher strategic view on many occasions, we must always remind ourselves that such lofty perspectives might be hidden or irrelevant to a young man struggling to make it alive to the end of the day in horrific circumstances. Witnessing the death or wounding of men running at extravagant levels of consumption, often for patches of seemingly insignificant land, could scarcely avoid cutting a deep wound into the French military psyche.

There were, nonetheless, reasons for the French to extract some confidence from the outcome of the Battle of Verdun. Chief amongst these was the utilisation of artillery, which the Verdun experience fine-tuned to new levels of efficiency. Creeping barrages, inching forward as a wall of steel just in front of an infantry advance (64m/70yds behind field gun shells, and 137m/150yds behind heavier howitzers), became expertly timed and were a key ingredient in the successes of the October and December offensives. The short distance between barrage and troops meant that the enemy did not have time to recuperate as the barrage lifted and the attacking troops crossed the remaining distance. Ironically, it was Nivelle who was central to the development of the French creeping barrage, and it was the failure of this tactic on the Aisne in April 1917 that was a significant contributory factor to the major French casualties there.

Another reason behind the final French victory was logistical. Pétain's logistical improvements have already been outlined above, and they ensured that both men and materiel kept flowing forward to sustain a significant defence. In total, the French fired some 23 million artillery shells, and transporting these alone to the

48. 'The growing pile' – cartoon depicting the effect of defeat at Verdun on 'Germany's hopes'. (The War Budget, 16 March 1916. Montreal Star)

artillery batteries at the right time, and with appropriate storage and handling, was a masterpiece of organisation. Logistics was the support on which the whole French effort rested, and those who performed its duties day in and day out, often under the pre-ranged attentions of German artillery, deserve enduring respect.

Beyond Verdun

The German defeats at Verdun in 1916 were not the end of fighting in the Verdun sector. The war still had two more years of agony ahead of it, and Verdun was not to be spared further suffering. The sector remained relatively quiet for the period January–August 1917. Then on 20 August 1917, French forces launched another major offensive, applying eight divisions and recapturing almost all of the features that remained in German hands from February 1916, including Regnéville, Samogeux and Hill 304. The offensive ran until early September, after which the Verdun sector descended into relative quiet once again. The final act came on 26 September 1918, this time with the energetic support of the US Army (the United States had declared war on Germany on 6 April 1917). The Franco-American Meuse-Argonne offensive saw American troops attack up the west bank of the Meuse, taking Malancourt, Béthincourt and Forges in short order, while the French Fourth Army advanced uncertainly up the right bank. The battle ran on until the very end of the war, and saw the French forces take the critical supply hub of Sedan on 6 November, five days before the Armistice. With the conclusion of hostilities on 11 November, the Verdun region could finally enjoy some measure of peace, and begin the long road to restoration.

THE LEGACY

Every year, thousands of people visit Verdun, drawn to the site of what is certainly one of human history's greatest battles. Many battlefields around the world have their lines etched only in the imagination, time obscuring the military positions with new vegetation or concrete. Verdun is different. Certainly the landscape there is much changed from 1916 – large areas have been cultivated with conifer trees, or planted with crops. Certain villages that artillery scoured from the earth in 1916 never returned to life; of Fleury, for example, all that stands today is a museum, a chapel and some memorial markers – the thriving village of around 400 inhabitants has truly gone for good.

Yet venture into the landscape around Fleury, Thiaumont or Douaumont, and the contours of the ground speak vividly of the shellfire that swept the region day after day. The terrain undulates constantly, each dip indicating a shell crater made by one or multiple explosions nearly a century ago (at the time of writing). The experience can be deepened by visiting the dank and haunting interior of Fort Douaumont or the shattered superstructure of Fort Vaux. All around the Verdun battle site, regular memorials, ranging from the grand to the humble, note

---

DID YOU KNOW?

Such was the intensity of the shellfire in the Verdun sector, that it has been calculated that every square metre of the battle area received a total of six shell or bomb impacts.

---

the human loss associated with almost every square metre of the region. A treacherous reminder of the war includes the dozens of unexploded shells unearthed from the landscape every year; for decades following the Great War, these were killing farmers with grim regularity, detonated typically when the blade of a plough struck the rusted casing.

Yet if there is a focal point to today's Verdun, it is the Douaumont cemetery and ossuary, the latter surmounted by a sombre 46m (151ft) high tower. The cemetery itself contains 16,142 graves, a small fraction of the hundreds of thousands of men who died in the battle. The ossuary, however, is filled with the bones of some 130,000 unidentified victims of the fighting, a particularly unnerving reminder of the sheer brutality of the effect shellfire has on the human frame. Officially inaugurated in 1932 (although under development from 1920), it is a haunting site that still makes an impression on modern visitors.

Such was the scale of what happened at Verdun, that it left a natural legacy in military thought and martial education. We should never forget that some key figures of the future Wehrmacht served as young officers at Verdun in 1916–18. They included: FM Friedrich von Paulus, Gen. Hans von Kluge, Gen. Karl-Heinrich von Stülpnagel, FM Wilhelm Keitel, Generaloberst Heinrich von Brauchitsch, Ernst Röhm and Rudolf Hess. They also included Generaloberst Heinz Guderian and FM Erich von Manstein, two of Germany's leading tactical thinkers in the Second World War and pioneers of mobile combined-arms manoeuvre warfare.

FORT DOUAUMONT, 20–23 MAY 1916

A French account of the battle

The valley separating Le Mort-Homme from Hill 287 is choked with bodies. A full brigade was mowed down in a quarter hour's holocaust by our machine guns. Le Mort-Homme itself passed from our possession, but the crescent Bourrus position to the south prevents the enemy from utilising it.

The scene there is appalling, but is dwarfed in comparison with fighting around Douaumont. West of the Meuse, at least, one dies in the open air, but at Douaumont is the horror of darkness, where the men fight in tunnels, screaming with the lust of butchery, deafened by shells and grenades, stifled by smoke.

Even the wounded refuse to abandon the struggle. As though possessed by devils, they fight on until they fall senseless from loss of blood. A surgeon in a front-line post told me that, in a redoubt at the south part of the fort, of 200 French dead, fully half had more than two wounds. Those he was able to treat seemed utterly insane. They kept shouting war cries and their eyes blazed, and, strangest of all, they appeared indifferent to pain.

Quoted in Horne, *Source Records*, 1923

Their frustration in 1944–45 is easy to imagine, as they found their tactical talents hobbled by their commander-in-chief, Adolf Hitler, who again frittered away thousands of lives with his stubborn refusal to relinquish ground.

When viewing Verdun from a tactical perspective, however, we should remember that the battle did introduce certain innovations that would affect either the conduct of the remaining years of the First World War, or conflicts after 1918. We have already considered the use of artillery, which Verdun confirmed as a battle-winning component of combined-arms warfare, if used with technological skill and adequate logistical support. Another point

*49. The burning debris of a German aeroplane destroyed by the French in the region of Verdun. (*The Illustrated War News, *24 May 1916)*

of interest was the role of aircraft in the battle. Verdun became one of the most active theatres on the Western Front for the tactical development of fighter aircraft. Although aircraft were primarily used for reconnaissance purposes at the beginning of the battle, by the mid point of 1916, German Fokker and French Nieuport fighters were regularly locked in aerial clashes over the battlefield. For the first quarter of the year, the Germans held the advantage, partly through the use of the formidable Fokker Eindeckker EI monoplane, with a machine-gun mounted on the engine cowling and synchronised to fire directly through the moving propeller without the bullets striking the blades. From March 1916 the Germans also pioneered more aggressive *Jadgstaffeln* (hunting flights), the fighters working in groups of six to nine aircraft and actively hunting down the French opponents rather than merely preventing them from penetrating German air space.

The air war became more balanced when the highly capable Nieuport 17 fighter, first introduced during the spring of 1916, began to enter service with the French *escadrilles* (squadrons). During April, the French retaliated against the 'Fokker scourge' with their own brand of aggressive flying, and during these clashes both sides established 'aces' with multiple kills to their names. Then, as summer turned to autumn, the Germans once again took the advantage with the introduction of the Albatros DII fighter, with its twin machine-guns. Only towards the end of the year, when French numerical superiority in the air took its effect, did the skies belong once more to the home nation. One other notable feature of the air war was that, from April 1916, American pilots were flying for the French side as part of the 'Escadrille Americaine'; the name was quickly changed for political reasons to 'Escadrille Lafayette', but these volunteers became famed both in Europe and back in the United States. They were also some of the first Americans to die in the First World War, losing their lives in a battle that established just how important aircraft could be to modern warfare.

Back on the ground, Verdun left a legacy in a new awareness of infantry tactics, on both sides of the frontline. The Germans realised that fast manoeuvre in small groups, the men utilising cover on the move and reliant upon small arms, grenades and flamethrowers, could be a deciding factor in the assault phase of operations. The German stormtrooper concept was tested and proved during the Battle of Verdun, and it would become a key ingredient of initial German successes during the offensives of 1918. It would also go on to inform the *Blitzkrieg* tactics of the Second World War.

The French also understood the importance of fast infantry manoeuvre, particularly in the context of the offensive spirit laid down by Grandmaison. However, the French took another lesson from Verdun, one that would have catastrophic consequences for the country in 1940.

By the summer of 1916 the French General Staff were somewhat in thrall to the fact that fortifications such as Fort Douaumont seemed to be standing up to the most crushing artillery punishment. In a dramatic reversal of pre-war military thinking, after the war the French strategists began to revisit the idea of men fighting from static, massive fortification complexes. In some ways the line of thinking was quite natural – German artillery barrages had proven that being out in the open landscape under a storm of shell was not a healthy place to be. Yet given the fact that many of the fortresses were eventually smashed (Douaumont was itself finally penetrated by the French railway guns), the tactical *volte face* was striking. Pétain himself came to acknowledge the resilience of the modern fortress, as he testified in his post-war volume *La Bataille de Verdun*:

> If from the beginning we had had confidence in the skill of our military engineers, the struggle before Verdun would have taken a different course. Fort Douaumont, occupied as it ought to have been, would not have been taken ... from the first it would have discouraged German ambitions. Fortification, what little there was of it, played a very large role in the victory.
>
> Quoted in Horne, *Price of Glory*, p.337

Pétain knew that the sheer human cost of Verdun had almost brought the country and certainly the army to its knees, and he saw an intelligent revisiting of the principles of fortification as an important step to avoiding such slaughter in the future. Pétain's views, supported by other influential thinkers amongst the French military camp, were the catalyst for the development of what became known as the Maginot Line, constructed 1930–40. The line was named after the French Minister of War André Maginot, himself a veteran of Verdun, and its physical layout was quite different to that of the Verdun fortifications. Running along the Franco-German border, the Maginot Line consisted of literally

THE LOSS OF FORTS DOUAUMONT AND VAUX, NOVEMBER 1916

Announcement by Erich Ludendorff

The forts of Douaumont and of Vaux played an important part in the battle of Verdun so long as they remained as French forts in the hands of the defenders. In order to weaken the Verdun position they had to be rendered inoffensive; deprived of their fighting means and largely destroyed, they possessed only a limited value for the assaulting party from a tactical point of view immediately the attack upon Verdun had been interrupted. Further, they gave the French artillery excellent objectives. In consequence of local gains by the French in the neighbourhood of the former Fort of Douaumont the importance of Vaux Fort to the German troops had become less than nil and there was no reason to make great sacrifices for the maintenance of this advanced position.

Quoted in Horne, *Source Records*, 1923

hundreds of blockhouses, pillboxes, retractable gun cupolas (these have proven themselves especially durable at Verdun), casemates and other steel and concrete fortifications, often linked by deep underground passages. Living conditions beneath the positions were improved with facilities such as air conditioning and even underground railways, to transfer men and materiel quickly between locations.

The Maginot Line gave the French an enormous protective confidence in the immediate months before the outbreak of the Second World War. It was seen as an impassable barrier, a safeguard of the French hinterlands from the Nazi war machine that had been swelling in scale since the ascent of Hitler in 1933. Tragically, while the under-investment in fortification proved to be a key French failing at Verdun, the over-investment in fortifications in the 1930s proved to be even more destabilising in 1940. In a campaign of strategic and tactical brilliance, German Panzer and mechanised units largely bypassed the entire Maginot Line by attacking through the Belgian Ardennes forest. The French and British forces were then consistently outmanoeuvred and outfought, and on 22 June – the Germans having already reached the French coast and taken Paris – a Franco-German armistice was signed. Pétain shattered his reputation forever by running

50. Section of the Maginot Line, 1944. (Author's collection)

the collaborationist Vichy government in the southern regions of France, a role that would permanently overshadow the service he had provided during the First World War. After the war, Pétain was sentenced to death for treason, although this sentence was commuted by Charles de Gaulle into life imprisonment, and the once great leader died on 23 July 1951.

It is interesting to note that when the Germans did attempt to take the Maginot Line in earnest, during Operation Tiger launched on 15 June by Army Group C, the fortifications proved as stubborn as they had been designed to be. Many of the strongest artillery positions were virtually impenetrable to German artillery. Assaults on individual positions cost the German troops heavy casualties, and in total only ten of the fifty-eight major fortifications in the line were actually taken in combat, despite these positions often having skeletal crews. In the end, the fall of the Maginot Line was more to do with the Germans encircling and isolating the line from the rest of France, making continued resistance there impractical and pointless.

Although the fabric of the Maginot Line had shown itself capable of resisting the best of modern artillery, what it could not handle was the new war of movement provided by armour and mechanisation. The Second World War would be about mobility – to be static was to be destroyed, especially once air power came of age in the form of effective long-range bombers with massive payloads or hard-hitting ground-attack aircraft.

The German campaign in the West in 1940 demonstrated how much warfare had changed in just over two decades. Never again would static concrete fortifications be key to the outcome of battles (intelligently positioned defensive field positions were another matter). If ever there was a poignant reflection of this it came with the surrender of Verdun to German forces on 15 June 1940. Fort Douaumont and Vaux, despite being upgraded during the interwar years, surrendered without serious resistance (Douaumont's guns didn't fire a single shot). For 200 casualties, most sustained on Hill 304 and Le Mort-Homme, and just twenty-four hours of fighting, the Germans took positions and terrain that had cost them hundreds of thousands of men twenty-four years previously.

The Battle of Verdun in 1916 has been offered by historians as one of the most costly engagements in human history. Certainly it has few rivals for the sheer concentration of horror and the intensity of the destruction. Such arguments, however, are a statistical deflection from the tragic heroism and profound sadness that surrounded this battle, a clash of arms that will continue to resonate through future history and the landscape around Verdun.

ORDERS OF BATTLE

German Order of Battle, 22 February 1916

VII Reserve Corps (General der Infanterie von Zwehl)

14th Reserve Division (Generalleutnant Loeb)
77th Infantry Brigade
>> 37th Fusilier Regiment
>> 5th Reserve Jäger Regiment (Regiment Major Freiherr von Stossingen)

27th Reserve Brigade
>> 16th Reserve Infantry Regiment
>> 159th Infantry Regiment

53rd Reserve Infantry Regiment (divisional reserve)

13th Reserve Division (General der Kavallerie von Kühne)
28th Reserve Brigade
>> 7th Reserve Infantry Regiment
>> 39th Reserve Infantry Regiment
>> 57th Reserve Infantry Regiment (in divisional reserve)

Corps Reserve
>> 13th Reserve Infantry Regiment
>> 18th Pioneer Regiment

7th Pioneer Regiment
283rd Reserve Pioneer Regiment
287th Reserve Pioneer Regiment

Artillery

1/13th Regiment
1/14th Regiment
23rd Foot Artillery Battalion
II/13th Reserve Field Artillery Regiment
II/5th Foot Artillery
7/13th Reserve Field Artillery
I/6th Foot Artillery
I/7th Foot Artillery
I/3rd Bayerische Foot Artillery
III/4th Foot Artillery
II/2nd Reserve Foot Artillery
III/18th Reserve Foot Artillery
II/14th Reserve Field Artillery
I/15th Reserve Field Artillery

XVIII Army Corps (General der Infanterie von Schend)

21st Infantry Division (Generalleutnant von Oven)
42nd Infantry Brigade
81st Infantry Regiment
87th Infantry Regiment

25th Infantry Division (Generalleutnant von Kühne)
49th Infantry Brigade
115th Leibgarde Infantry Regiment
117th Infantry Regiment
Reserve Guard Pioneer Regiment

Corps Reserve
80th Fusilier Regiment

116th Infantry Regiment
286th Reserve Pioneer Regiment
30th Reserve Pioneer Regiment

Artillery

I/25th Field Artillery
II/25th Field Artillery
II/61st Field Artillery
I/61st Field Artillery
6/10th Reserve Field Artillery
6/9th Reserve Field Artillery
III/14th Reserve Foot Artillery
I/3rd Foot Artillery
III/7th Foot Artillery
II/9th Foot Artillery
I/9th Foot Artillery
III/14th Foot Artillery
II/6th Reserve Foot Artillery
220th Foot Artillery Battalion
223rd Foot Artillery Battalion
I/10th Field Artillery
II/63rd Field Artillery
I/27th Field Artillery

III Army Corps (General der Infanterie von Lochow)

5th Infantry Division (Generalleutnant Wishura)
10th Infantry Brigade
8th Leib-Grenadier Regiment
12th Grenadier Regiment

6th Infantry Division (Generalleutnant von Rohden)
12th Infantry Brigade
24th Infantry Regiment
64th Infantry Regiment

3rd Infantry Regiment (as divisional reserve)

Corps Reserve
>52nd Infantry Regiment
>20th Infantry Regiment
>23rd Pioneer Regiment

Artillery
>5th Field Artillery Brigade
>18th Field Artillery Regiment
>6th Field Artillery Brigade
>13th Field Artillery Regiment
>39th Field Artillery Regiment
>II/16th Reserve Foot Artillery
>I/16th Reserve Foot Artillery
>I/2nd Garde-Foot Artillery
>216th Bayerische Foot Artillery
>II/8th Reserve Foot Artillery
>27th Foot Artillery Battalion
>III/20th Reserve Foot Artillery
>II/20th Foot Artillery
>II/7th Reserve Foot Artillery
>III/3rd Reserve Foot Artillery
>I/11th Foot Artillery
>IV/1st Foot Artillery
>I/12th Foot Artillery
>I/9th Reserve Foot Artillery

German Divisions in Verdun sector, March–September 1916. Left bank of the Meuse:

Angriffsgruppe West (General der Artillerie von Gallwitz General der Infanterie von Francois)

VI Reserve Corps (General von Gossler)
>   11th Bavarian Division
>   192nd Infantry Brigade
>   11th Reserve Division
>   12th Reserve Division
>   22nd Reserve Division

XXII Reserve Corps (Cavalry General von Falkenhayn)
>   43rd Reserve Division
>   44th Reserve Division
>   56th Infantry Division
>   4th Infantry Division

XXIV Reserve Corps (General der Infanterie General von Gerof)
>   38th Infantry Division
>   54th Infantry Division

Right bank of the Meuse

Angriffsgruppe Mudra, 19 March–16 April (General von Mudra)

Angriffsgruppe Ost, 16 April onwards (General von Lochow)

X Reserve Corps (General Kosch)
>   19th Reserve Division
>   58th Infantry Division
>   113rd Infantry Division

I Bayerische Army Corps (General Ritter von Inlander)
>   1st Bavarian Division
>   2nd Bavarian Division

Alpen Corps (Generalleutnant von Dellmensingen)
>   4th Infantry Division
>   14th Infantry Division

33rd Infantry Division
34th Infantry Division
6th Bavarian Division

X Reserve Corps
7th Infantry Division
103rd Infantry Division
25th Reserve Division

French Order of Battle, 22 February–4 March 1916

Army Group Centre (General Herr/General Pétain)

XXX Army Corps (General Chrétien)

72nd Reserve Division (General Bapst)
143rd Brigade
351st Regiment
362nd Regiment
56th Chasseurs à Pied
59th Chasseurs à Pied
1st Battalion, 44th Territorial Regiment

144th Brigade
164th Regiment
165th Regiment

107th Brigade
324th Regiment
365th Regiment

Cavalry
2nd Hussars (1 squadron)

Artillery

> 1 Group – 1 battery each from 11th, 41st, 45th, 59th, 61st Regiments
> 109th Battery from 61st Regiment

51st Reserve Division (General Boullangé)

101st Brigade

> 233rd Regiment
> 243rd Regiment
> 327th Regiment
> 1 Battalion, 29th Territorial Regiment

102nd Brigade

> 208th Regiment
> 273rd Regiment
> 310th Regiment

Cavalry

> 11e Hussars (2 squadrons)

Artillery

> 1 Group – 1 battery each from 15th, 27th, 41st and 107th Regiments
> 107th Battery, 15th Regiment

106th Territorial Division (General Bierren)

211st Territorial Brigade

> 15th Territorial Regiment
> 44th Territorial Regiment
> 45th Territorial Regiment

212th Territorial Brigade

> 46th Territorial Regiment
> 48th Territorial Regiment
> 95th Territorial Regiment

132th Division (General Renaud)
108th Brigade
>>303rd Regiment
>>330th Regiment
>>364th Regiment

264th Brigade
>>66th Regiment
>>166th Regiment (4 battalions)

Cavalry
>>1st Hussars (2 squadrons)

Artillery
>>1 Group – 3 batteries of 57th Regiment
>>1 Group – 1 battery each from 4th, 22nd, 48th and 101st Regiments
>>101st Battery, 17th Regiment

Engineers
>>4 companies

Corps Artillery

>>1 Group – 1 battery each from 17th, 36th and 48th Regiments
>>102nd and 114th Heavy Artillery Regiments

VII Army Corps (General de Bazelaire)

14th Division (General Crépen)
27th Brigade
>>42nd Regiment
>>44th Regiment

Artillery

>3 Groups – 47th Regiment

37th Division (General de Bonneval)
73rd Brigade

>2nd Zouaves
>2nd Algerian Tirailleurs

Cavalry

>11th Chasseurs à Cheval (2 squadrons)

Artillery

>3 Groups from African artillery regiments

Cavalry

>11e Chasseurs à Cheval (4 squadrons)

Artillery

>1 Group – 107th Heavy Regiment
>103rd Battery, 5th Regiment

XX Army Corps (General Balfourier)

153rd Division (General Deligny)
306th Brigade

>418th Regiment
>2th Battalion Chasseurs à Pied
>4th Battalion Chasseurs à Pied
>3rd Maross Brigade
>1 Mixed Regiment – 2 battalions Algerian Tirailleurs;
>1/1 Zouaves
>9th Zouave Regiment

Artillery

>2 Groups – 60th Regiment

Half of 108th Battery, 60th Regiment

39th Division (General Rourrisson)
77th Brigade
> 146th Regiment
> 153rd Regiment

78th Brigade
> 156th Regiment
> 160th Regiment

Cavalry
> 5th Hussars (1 squadron)

Artillery
> 3 Groups – 39th Regiment

Cavalry
> 5th Hussars (4 squadrons)

Artillery
> 2 Groups – 60th Regiment
> 1 Group – 120th Heavy Regiment
> 108th Battery, 60th Regiment

I Army Corps (General Guillaumat)

1st Division (General de Riols de Fonclare)
1st Brigade
> 43rd Regiment
> 127th Regiment

2nd Brigade
> 1st Regiment
> 201st Regiment

Artillery

>3 Groups – 15th Regiment

2nd Division (General Guignahaudet)
3rd Brigade

>33rd Regiment
>73rd Regiment

3rd Brigade

>8th Regiment
>10th Regiment

Artillery

>3 Groups – 27th Regiment

Cavalry

>6th Chasseurs à Cheval (4 squadrons)

Artillery

>2 Groups – 41st Regiment
>1 Group – 101st Heavy Regiment

Divisions not subordinated to Corps HQs

16th Division (General Rouquerol)
31st Brigade

>85th Regiment
>95th Regiment

32nd Brigade

>13th Regiment
>29th Regiment

Artillery

>3 Groups – 1st Regiment

48th Division (General Capdepont)
95th Brigade
      170th Regiment
      174th Regiment

96th Brigade (newly established)
      2nd Mixed Regiment (Zouaves and Algerian Tirailleurs)
      Moroccan Regiment

Artillery
      2 Groups – 5th Regiment
      1 Group – 19th Regiment

Douaumont–Vaux Sector, June–July 1916

12th Division
23rd Brigade
      54th Infantry Regiment
      67th Infantry Regiment

24th Brigade
      106th Infantry Regiment
      132nd Infantry Regiment

127th Division
253rd Brigade
      172nd Infantry Regiment
      25th Battalion Chasseurs à Pied
      29th Battalion Chasseurs à Pied

254th Brigade
171st Infantry Regiment
      19th Battalion Chasseurs à Pied
      26th Battalion Chasseurs à Pied

52nd Division

103rd Brigade

     291st Infantry Regiment

     347th Infantry Regiment

     348th Infantry Regiment

104th Brigade

     245th Infantry Regiment

     320th Infantry Regiment

     49th Battalion Chasseurs à Pied

63rd Division

125th Brigade

     216th Infantry Regiment

     238th Infantry Regiment

     298th Infantry Regiment

126th Brigade

     292nd Infantry Regiment

     305th Infantry Regiment

     321st Infantry Regiment

124th Division

247th Brigade

     101st Infantry Regiment

     124th Infantry Regiment

248th Brigade

     53rd Infantry Regiment

     142nd Infantry Regiment

130th Division

260th Brigade

     39th Infantry Regiment

     239th Infantry Regiment

307th Brigade

      405th Infantry Regiment

      407th Infantry Regiment

131st Division

261st Brigade

      41st Infantry Regiment

      241st Infantry Regiment

262nd Brigade

      7th Infantry Regiment

      14th Infantry Regiment

71st Division

141st Brigade

      368th Infantry Regiment

      370th Infantry Regiment

142nd Brigade

      217th Infantry Regiment

      221st Infantry Regiment

128th Division

255th Brigade

      167th Infantry Regiment

      168th Infantry Regiment

256th Brigade

      169th Infantry Regiment

      100th Infantry Regiment

16th Division

31st Brigade

      85th Infantry Regiment

      95th Infantry Regiment

32nd Brigade
>> 13th Infantry Regiment
>> 29th Infantry Regiment

154th Division
308th Brigade
>> 41st Colonial Regiment
>> 43rd Colonial Regiment

309th Brigade
>> 413rd Infantry Regiment
>> 414th Infantry Regiment

Attached territorial regiments: 5th, 6th, 7th, 50th, 110th, 98th, 97th, 112th and 17th

131st Artillery Division
>> 1st Group
>> 2nd Group
>> 3rd Group

130th Artillery Division
>> 3rd Group

127th Artillery Division
>> 3rd Group
>> 4th Group
>> 5th Group

Heavy Artillery
>> 106th Regiment/8th Group
>> 116th Regiment/8th Group
>> 104th Regiment/7th Group
>> 107th Regiment/7th Group

Field Artillery
12th Artillery Division (25th Regiment)
      1st Group
      2nd Group
      3rd Group

C6 Artillery
      3rd Group
      5th Group

Army Level Artillery:

Field Artillery
      11th Regiment
      46th Regiment

Heavy Artillery
      81st Regiment/9th Group
      107th Regiment/ 5th Group
      107th Regiment/6th Group
      5th Regiment/ 5th Group
      28th Regiment/1st Group

Army Artillery
      115th Regiment/3rd Group
      81st Regiment/5th Group
      81st Regiment/6th Group
      106th Regiment/5th Group

Naval Artillery
      84th Regiment/6th Group
      103rd Regiment/1st Group
      103rd Regiment/5th Group

African Foot Artillery
      6th Group
      83rd Regiment
      82nd Regiment

French Troops in the Souville Sector, May–October 1916

III Corps (Lebrun)
36th Division
      71st Brigade
      72nd Brigade

124th Division
      247th Brigade
      248th Brigade

6th Division
      11th Brigade
      12th Brigade

52nd Division
      103rd Brigade
      104th Brigade

130th Division
      260th Brigade
      307th Brigade

VI Corps (Paulinier)
131st Division
      261st Brigade
      262nd Brigade

128th Division
>> 255th Brigade
>> 256th Brigade

33rd Division
>> 65th Brigade
>> 66th Brigade

37th Division
>> 73rd Brigade
>> 74th Brigade

15th Division
>> 29th Brigade
>> 30th Brigade

38th Division
>> 76th Brigade
>> 4th Moroccan Brigade

32nd Division
>> 63rd Brigade
>> 64th Brigade

68th Division
>> 135th Brigade
>> 136th Brigade

67th Division
>> 133rd Brigade
>> 134th Brigade

133rd Division
>> 115th Brigade
>> 214th Brigade
>> 314th Brigade

14th Division
>>27th Brigade
>>28th Brigade

63rd Division
>>125th Brigade
>>126th Brigade

VI Corps (Paulinier)
12th Division
>>23rd Brigade
>>24th Brigade

127th Division
>>253rd Brigade
>>24th Brigade

127th Division
>>253rd Brigade
>>254th Brigade

71st Division
>>141st Brigade
>>142nd Brigade

16th Division
>>31st Brigade
>>32nd Brigade

XIV Corps (Baret)
154th Division
>>308th Brigade
>>309th Brigade

27th Division
>> 53rd Brigade
>> 54th Brigade

73rd Division
>> 145th Brigade
>> 146th Brigade

74th Division
>> 147th Brigade
>> 148th Brigade

XII Corps (Nollet)
56th Division
>> 111st Brigade
>> 112nd Brigade

154th Division
>> 308th Brigade
>> 309th Brigade

28th Division
>> 55th Brigade
>> 56th Brigade

151st Division
>> 301st Brigade
>> 302nd Brigade

21st Division
>> 41st Brigade
>> 42nd Brigade

Groupment D (established 19 June)

II Corps (Mangin) replaced XII Corps (Nollet) 22 June
129th Division
>257th Brigade
>258th Brigade

60th Division
>119th Brigade
>120th Brigade

8th Division
>15th Brigade
>16th Brigade

31st Division
>61st Brigade
>62nd Brigade

19th Division
>37th Brigade
>38th Brigade

7th Division
>13th Brigade
>14th Brigade

55th Division
>109th Brigade
>110th Brigade

FURTHER READING

Books

Asprey, Robert B., *The German High Command at War* (New York, W. Morrow, 1991)

Brown, Malcolm, *Verdun 1916* (Stroud, The History Press, 2003)

Buckingham, William F., *Verdun 1916: Battlefield Guide* (Stroud, Tempus, 2007)

Carey, John (ed.), *Eyewitness to History* (New York, Avon Books, 1987)

Donnell, Clayton, *The Fortifications of Verdun* (Oxford, Osprey, 2011)

Drury, Ian, *German Stormtrooper 1914–18* (Oxford, Osprey, 1995)

von Falkenhayn, General Erich, *The German General Staff and its decisions 1914–16* (New York, 1920)

Fosten, D.S.V and R.J. Marrion, *The German Army 1914–18* (Oxford, Osprey, 1978)

Gilbert, Martin, *The First World War: A Complete History* (London, Phoenix Press, 2000)

Horne, Alastair, *The Price of Glory: Verdun 1916* (London, Penguin, 1962)

Horne, Charles F. (ed.), *Source Records of the Great War* (London, 1923)

Keegan, John, *The First World War* (London, Pimlico, 1999)

Martin, William, *Verdun 1916: 'They Shall Not Pass'* (Oxford, Osprey, 2001)

McConnell, James R., *Flying for France* (New York, 1916)

Ousby, Ian, *The Road to Verdun* (London, Jonathan Cape, 2002)

Romains, Jules, *Verdun* (London, Prion Books, 1999)

Saunders, Anthony, *The Weapons of Trench Warfare 1914–18* (Stroud, Sutton Publishing, 2000)

Sumner, Ian, *French Poilu 1914–18* (Oxford, Osprey, 2009)

Wilmott, H.P., *World War I* (London, Dorling Kindersley, 2009)

Wukovits, John, *World War I: Strategic Battles* (Farmington Hills, MI, Lucent Books, 2001)

Useful websites:

firstworldwar.com: Major First World War website with extensive coverage of Verdun, including primary source documents: http://www.firstworldwar.com/battles/verdun.htm

World War One battlefields: A battlefield tourism website with interesting photographic section on Verdun: http://www.ww1battlefields.co.uk/verdun.html

Douaumont Ossuary: The official website of this important Verdun memorial: http://www.verdun-douaumont.com/en/index.html

Places to visit

Interesting locations on the Verdun battlefield:

• Camp Marguerre – approx. 16km (10 miles) north-west of Verdun, signposted from the D16 from village of Loisin

- Douaumont Ossuary and cemetery – off the D193 near Thiaumont
- Fort Douaumont – signposted off the D193 north-west of Verdun
- Douaumont Village – remains of the destroyed village, near Fort Douaumont itself
- Memorial Museum – located at what had been the village of Fleury. The village itself (of which nothing remains) was immediately behind the memorial
- Fort Vaux – Located east and south of the D112
- Haucourt Village – on the D18 approx. 16km (10 miles) north-west of Verdun
- Hill 304 – off the D18 north of Esnes
- Le Mort-Homme – off the D123 near Chattancourt

Memorial of Verdun

1, Avenue du Corps Européen
55100 Fleury-devant-Douaumont
Tel. : +33 (0)3 29 84 35 34
Fax : +33 (0)3 29 84 45 54
E-mail : Memorial.14-18@wanadoo.fr

Web: http://www.memorialdeverdun.fr/index.php/index_uk.html

INDEX

Index

Index